VICTIMS MAKE
THE BEST
BIRDHOUSES

VICTIMS MAKE THE BEST BIRDHOUSES

LARRY L. FRANKLIN

E.L. Marker
Salt Lake City

Published by E.L. Marker, an imprint of WiDo Publishing

WiDo Publishing
Salt Lake City, Utah
widopublishing.com

Cover design by Steven Novak
Book design by Marny K. Parkin

ISBN 978-1-947966-57-4

Note from the Author

It is not my job to convince you that I am a victim of physical and sexual abuse. I share my journey, leaving you to draw your own conclusions. While my story is based on what I believe to be true, I recognize the possibility of minor discrepancies in human recall. It is my hope that fellow victims of physical and sexual abuse will benefit from my sharing and become stronger and wiser than before.

To my therapist

*Once in a lifetime
you meet someone who changes
everything.*

Trauma is a vampire, but light, as any student of folklore or Freud knows, will kill it. The problem is, when the shell-shocked try to exhume their memories—to bring them into the light—the result can be a death struggle so fierce they may fear it's them, not the suckling pain that's about to die.

—Katherine Russell Rich
The Red Devil: A Memoir About Beating The Odds

DID YOU LOVE ME JUST A LITTLE?

I sat with my mother
in my grandpa's 1949 Chevy.
I don't remember feeling,
Just knowing
That I'd been thrown away.
My parents had broken up the night before.
That morning, Dad decided
Who would stay
And who would go.
The "runt of the litter,"
Always last,
Never seen, and always passed,
Sat with his mother in the 1949 Chevy.
Oh, Dad, I wished you were alive,
So I could ask.
Did you love me just a little?

—Larry L. Franklin

PROLOGUE

I SHOULD HAVE KNOWN ON THAT SUMMER DAY IN 1950 when my seven-year-old naked body was laid out over a bale of hay that this was not normal. I should have known. But I was the youngest and smallest of four boys in a place where the unspeakable was normal. Even at this very young age, my brain was forced to compartmentalize daily interactions, whether they be good, bad, or indifferent. The horrific ones were hidden for decades as secrets never meant to be revealed.

In 1992, a chance conversation with my mother opened the door to repressed memories. The worst ones left me hugging my bathroom stool while vomiting throughout the night. As my mind began to crumble, a piece here, a piece there, I learned that the trips to the barn were far from normal. But who would believe such a tale? Separating fact from fiction was like finding a gnat in the forest.

Early into therapy, I shared a repressed memory with a friend and told her that I was working with a therapist. I thought I would get a supportive reaction, but instead, I got something I wasn't expecting.

"I think you should get a different therapist," my friend said. "Some therapists plant false memories into your head."

I was stunned by her cold, matter-of-fact response. Unfortunately, her reaction was typical of the time. Public doubt about repressed memories in the 1990s was strong. This doubt and my reluctance to believe the unbelievable added to my anxieties and likely added years to my struggles.

My journey was a long one and not without risk. I was a vagabond wandering in an emotional wilderness. What sort of creatures might I find? Would they suck my soul dry? Would I find my way out?

Not long ago, I had cataract surgery. The next day, I removed my sunglasses and stared at a pear tree full of white blossoms that stood in front of our red-brick house. The shapes and colors appeared as three-dimensional figures, and the intense hues and minute details were unlike anything I had seen before. My emotional healing was no less dramatic. Years of therapy allowed me to feel in the same way that cataract surgery allowed me to see.

It has taken me twenty-five years to tell my story.

PART I
MEMORIES LAID BARE

Revelations

Friday the 23rd.

It was six-thirty in the morning and cold. I traveled north on Interstate 57 before reaching the blacktop that skirts Xenia, Oskaloosa, and Kinmundy on the way to my mother's house in Louisville. I had driven up from Makanda in silence. Seldom did I turn the radio on during these trips. Music was for the drive back.

I passed a gas station and the Louisville Cafe where men drink coffee and talk politics. As I drove past North Clay High, where I'd attended school, my breathing became shallow. To calm myself, I thought back to one of the finer memories of my childhood—the day my mother told me that I could have my own bed.

I was twelve and had slept with my mother since I was five years old. Each night I held onto the edge of our bed with a radio next to my ear. I prayed that her body would not touch mine. She always told me that we couldn't afford to buy another bed, but then one day she changed her mind. She took me to the local furniture store. There were all types of headboards, but the one that caught my eye had three shelves where I could store books, photos, or whatever I chose. It even came with a reading light that could be attached to one of the shelves. I told her this was the bed I wanted, and she bought it. I was so happy to have my own bed that I began giggling.

Even as a grown man, this memory brought a smile to my face, and when I pulled into my mother's driveway, my breathing had calmed.

It was not yet seven o'clock. The air was cold, and the sky was dark, but even in the dim light, I could see the foliage that colored my mother's yard like the fabric in her patchwork quilts. I knocked on the door of her small two-bedroom home and let myself in.

My mother was sitting in her chair in the living room, thumbing through an issue of *Country Woman*. I don't remember a time when she wasn't ready. Most of the time, she had her jacket on before my arrival. She looked up at me as I sat down.

"Hi, Larry. The weather has changed. You'll need a jacket if you're going outside."

I adjusted the Southern Illinois University hoodie I was wearing, "Well," I said, "I'm comfortable with this on. It's a heavy sweatshirt."

She looked back down at her magazine. "How are the girls?"

"They're doing fine. You know, getting ready for Halloween."

She nodded as if she understood.

My eyes shifted to the quilt-making frame that stood in the corner of the living room. Each Thursday, the frame was moved to the center of the room, allowing space for my mother, grandmother, and four church ladies to sit around it while quilting, talking, and sharing the latest gossip. The finished quilts were then passed on to the church for fund-raising purposes.

"You sure you don't want a coat?" she asked again. "It's chilly outside."

"No thank you, I'll be fine." After a brief pause, I asked, "What time do we need to be there?"

"Well, it happens at 8 o'clock."

"I see. Well, we'll need to get you there a little early because they'll need to check you in, and there'll probably be insurance papers to fill out. You know."

"Yes, I suppose you're right." My mother put down her magazine. "How long do you think it will take?"

"Oh, not too long. They said it's a simple procedure. I imagine you'll be back by the afternoon, depending on how long it takes for the doctors to sign off on everything. You know how it is."

She nodded again.

"The hospital's in Effingham, so if we leave now, we can be there in plenty of time."

"Okay," she said and rose from her chair. "Okay, let's go."

There was always a level of tension when my mother and I had a conversation. I didn't know why. When my wife was present, she absorbed most of the discussion. I observed the give-and-take between the two and added a word at strategic moments to let them know I was not asleep. Today I was on my own.

It was early Friday afternoon when we returned from the hospital in Effingham to my mother's home in Louisville. The surgery had gone well, and the doctor was pleased with the outcome. My mother was in good spirits and had asked that we stop at Martin's grocery store to pick up some food for dinner. As I stood in the kitchen unpacking the food, I overheard a string of telephone calls.

"Hello," my mother answered. "We just returned from the hospital. Surgery was fine. Yes, that's right. Larry came up early this morning and will be spending the night." Each call required a summary of the ordeal, including tales of the drafty hospital gown, the surgery, hospital food, and how the surgeon, Dr. Bucannon, was "such a nice man." As she spoke, she fingered the large gauze patch over her left eye. My mother was a small woman, no more than five feet tall, who sported a medium-cut head of hair that barely touched the bottom of her neck. If there was anything unusual about her appearance, it was her eyes. They were light green, I think. While she loved to tell a story and enjoyed a good laugh, her eyes seemed to be on a different journey. That afternoon was no different. As my mother chatted with her friends, her uncovered right eye seemed empty. In all fairness, maybe my eyes looked the same.

Once the food was set out and the phone quieted, I sat at the table and suggested that we eat something. No sooner had we begun when Reverend Robbins called.

"Yes, cataract surgery. I feel pretty good. But I don't feel perfect. It was quite an ordeal, you know. And it was hard on my nerves. Yes, Larry is here. You should see the meal he fixed." She talked about the crisp chicken, the creamy potato soup, and how the whipped cream was low fat. She neglected to mention that it was all ready-made from Martin's, and that I had served everything on paper plates.

After supper, we moved into the living room, where I quickly grabbed the La-Z-Boy recliner that had been my grandfather's favorite chair. I remember him sitting in that chair with his left hand holding an empty pork and bean can for his tobacco juice. His right hand held a small transistor radio broadcasting the latest St. Louis Cardinals baseball game with an earpiece stuck into his left ear. And at the same time, his right ear listened to the TV blasting out the latest episode of *Perry Mason*. If the game became overly exciting, he might miss the can, leaving some tobacco juice on the chair. Those were the times when my grandmother aired her dissatisfaction. Despite any shortcomings he may have had, I loved this man and called him Pop.

My mother sat in her favorite chair, surrounded by everything that she might need. On her left were knitting needles with yarn of various colors, the latest copy of *Country Woman,* and a book of circle-the-word puzzles. On the end-table to her right was a lamp, TV guide, remote control, cordless phone, and her Bible with pages folded to mark her favorite scriptures.

That night, my mother seemed more animated than usual. Perhaps it was the medication administered during the eye surgery that morning, but she spoke quickly with little regard to what she was saying. We were talking about the weather, a favorite topic of hers, when she asked if I remembered the hard winters on the farm in De Land, Illinois, where we had lived with my father and brother until I was seven.

Since my mother never talked about those years, her question startled me. I told her I didn't remember when our family lived in De Land, Illinois.

"Really?" My mother seemed surprised. "You don't remember anything?"

"I remember a couple of things about my dad," I said, "but I don't recall the hard winters on the farm."

My dad and brother had died in a car wreck when I was in second grade, and afterward, I had asked my mother to share memories of my dad. But my inquiries were always met with a crying spell followed by a change of topics. It only took a few attempts before I lost hope, concluding that I would never know my dad. Instead, I began imagining what my dad might have said, how he carried himself when he walked across the bean field, and if he was as strong as my uncle said. When meeting a man of admirable qualities, I would assume he was like my dad. *Yes, that's what my dad was like,* I would think, and I would add these qualities to my memories of a dad I never knew.

My mother paused. "Do you remember anything about your brother?"

All I knew about my brother was his name, Keith. I didn't remember anything about him. I didn't remember my brother showing me how to throw a curveball or slide into second base, how to tie a square knot, or how to put a worm on a fishing hook. I told my mother this.

"Well, I guess I shouldn't be too surprised. I've read where sometimes people can't remember bad things that happened to them. When I think about all the times your brother used to beat you, I can understand why you would want to forget it."

"What are you talking about?" I leaned forward in my chair.

"Your brother used to cut switches from the grove of hickory trees that stood just north of the farmhouse. He'd beat you until he left those big bloody welts all over your body."

This seemed unbelievable. "After all of these years, you're telling me that my brother used to beat me? If he was so bad, why didn't you stop him?"

"Well, when I tried, he'd beat me too. Sometimes he'd hit me in the stomach with his fists."

"Why didn't Dad stop him?" Surely she couldn't answer this question without hearing how ridiculous her accusations sounded.

My mother's face turned cold as she stared into the floor. "I told your dad what was going on. Lots of times.

I had you undress, so he could see those marks on your body. But he didn't care about you, not a bit. Your dad didn't love you."

For the moment, I was unable to speak. My mother had rolled an emotional grenade that spun on the gray carpet stretched out across the living room floor and came to a stop at my feet. Mentally, I threw my body on top of the grenade, hoping to stop the pain that twisted and churned in my body.

My voice trembled. "Are you telling me that Dad didn't love me?"

"Oh, he probably loved you. He must've. He just didn't want to be around you. I mean, he didn't have time for you." She was doing a poor job of reeling in her claims, even raising the pitch of her voice in a slightly humorous way. "Everybody said your dad and Keith were as close as a tick on a hound dog. Yes, Keith was his favorite."

We both sat in silence while staring at the television. I craved more information. "Did you ever have a good relationship with Dad?"

"Oh yes. The first few years were great. We worked hard on the farm but always found time for Saturday night dances at Farmer City, north of De Land. Of course, there were times when your dad drank too much, and I certainly didn't approve of that. Sometimes we'd play cards with Uncle James and Aunt Wanda. I liked them a lot. Things were pretty good then."

"Well, what happened? What changed?"

Looking up and off to the side, she drew memories out of the air. "I guess it was shortly after you were born. You were nine-and-a-half pounds and caused me some problems. I ended up having some female stuff that later required surgery. With me weighing only ninety-five pounds, you were a bit much for me. At first, I had to bring in some help to take care of you. I remember sitting on the couch as you scooted across the floor and ended up at my feet. You reminded me of a baby bird with his mouth open wide, wings flapping about, and crying to be held. I was just too weak to lift you. I guess that's when your dad and I grew apart. He began going to town each night, drinking and looking for other women."

She spoke these words as if I were to blame for her difficult pregnancy, subsequent surgery, broken marriage, and that I'd looked like an obese bird scooting across the floor.

"And then there were the night problems between you and Keith."

"Night problems? What kind of problems are you talking about?"

"Well, when you were four, Keith bothered you at night. He wouldn't let you sleep. He did bad things to you. So your dad said that Keith would sleep with him, and I would sleep with you. That's the way it was for the final four years of our marriage. But it wasn't my idea," she said as she raised her voice. "It was your dad's. Anyway, during those days, it was okay for parents to sleep with their kids. I guess it's different nowadays."

My mother's statement brought back a decades-old memory of a conversation I'd heard between her and a female friend when I was twelve. My mother had mentioned that she was sleeping with me, and her friend questioned whether a mother should be sleeping with her twelve-year-old son. The friend expressed concern that it could cause some emotional problems for me. I had always wondered what prompted my mother to change her mind about getting me my own bed. Was it this conversation with her friend I had forgotten until now? Suddenly, my mind flashed from this newly remembered conversation from almost forty years ago to a troubling moment with my mother just that morning. After checking into the hospital, she was handed a hospital gown and told to place her clothes in the locker and wear the gown. I was asked to help her if needed. While I felt awkward being in this situation, I agreed, and the nurse left the room. The awkwardness quickly escalated when my mother, instead of retreating behind the privacy screen to change, removed her clothing in front of me, and while completely naked, slipped into the gown. I was shocked at how casually she had exposed herself to me.

I pushed both memories away and turned my attention back to my mother. Her uncovered eye was filled with tears. I couldn't help but wonder if crying might be detrimental to her other eye, so I changed the subject by asking if it was time for the evening news. She nodded yes, and the two of us stared at the television set.

After the news ended, we went to our separate beds for the night. The next morning, we drove to the Louisville Cafe, the only restaurant in town. Men circled several tables, talked about politics and the weather, drank black coffee, and took deep pulls from their cigarettes. Two couples occupied separate tables: one with a child and one without. My mother and I ate one of our morning favorites—biscuits and gravy. We spoke little, certainly nothing of value, and the food was bland. I held the words from last night's conversation deep down in my stomach, hoping to finish breakfast without vomiting on the floor.

———

Saturday the 24th.

It was ten o'clock on Saturday before I was on US-45 South, headed home. After breakfast, I'd driven my mother back to her house and walked her to the front door. I'd asked her if she was sure she would be okay, and she'd assured me she would. She'd told me to say hello to the girls and Paula, and I'd promised I would. Then we separated. There was no hugging or kissing; we were a family that practiced social distancing even in the absence of illness.

Makanda was two hours away, and I wanted to be home soon. I'd never wanted to make this trip in the first place. I'd been running for a few years and had done the half-marathon in Chicago a few times and even the annual St. Louis marathon. This year I'd turned fifty, which placed me in a new age group, providing a better chance of winning a trophy. But seven days ago, my mother called to say she was having cataract surgery on Friday. She had asked me to accompany her to the hospital and spend the night at her house while she recovered.

I was scheduled to run a half-marathon in Cape Girardeau, Missouri, that Sunday. I could have told her no. I could have told her I had plans that weekend, and if she wanted my help, she should have contacted me before scheduling the procedure. But that was my mother. She did what she wanted, and if I hesitated, she invoked the mother's shame: "I'd be ashamed if I were you. God would want you to do the right thing." I never said no to her.

So I made the trip, even though it had disrupted the careful training I'd planned for the days leading to the race. Fortunately, Cape Girardeau was only an hour from Makanda, and if I could get home early enough, I'd have time to relax, go to bed, and get to the race on Sunday morning.

My mother never asked why I had to be home by Saturday, and I didn't tell her. She didn't know about my running. She would have considered it a silly thing for a grown man to do. My job was to provide her with grandchildren and provide my family with a comfortable living. My wife, Paula, and I had two daughters who loved their grandma. I ran my own financial planning business in southern Illinois, and Paula was an elementary teacher. That was all my mother cared to know.

I'd never felt so relieved, and at the same time void of feeling, as I did when I left her house on that stone-cold October day. As I began the two-hour drive back home, I kept the radio off. I was not in the mood for music. My body felt as if it were wrapped in a cocoon that was both protective and suffocating. I was dimly aware of the faint sound of rolling tires and an air leak that whistled around the window's edge. Some fifteen miles west of Louisville and no more than a mile to the interstate, my body began to shake. Tears ran down my face, and a layer of sweat covered my body. I rolled the front windows down; cold air blew across my face; my hands gripped the steering wheel that directed me to the shoulder of the blacktop road. I sat there as cars raced by, and I cried. These were unfamiliar emotions for me, the man who never cried. The image of my dad had been reduced to rubble. I wailed like a wounded animal.

I sat in my parked car for about fifteen minutes, wondering how I could complete the trip home. It was obvious that I would need all my strength and determination. I recalled the effort I'd needed during my last marathon, running the final six miles in freezing rain. It had been so cold that I prayed for a race-ending injury so I could stop. My prayers had gone unanswered, and I finished the race. The only thing that was going to get me home was me. I gripped the steering wheel, shifted into drive, and merged onto the interstate. The car accelerated from 30 mph to 50, then to 70, 80, 90 mph. Getting to the safety of my home in the fastest time possible was the prevailing logic.

Our bi-level home was just off Highway 51, so in less than three minutes after exiting the highway, I was pulling into our garage. My hands shook as I removed the keys and walked into the house. My dog PJ jumped up and down to greet me, my wife embraced me, and the bet-you-can't-make-me-cry man broke into tears.

"Larry! What's going on? Are you okay?"

I couldn't speak. I struggled to walk.

Paula rushed over and took my arm to steady me. "You're chalk-white, Larry. What happened? Were you in an accident?"

I was crying, deep heaving sobs, and couldn't speak, but I shook my head. This seemed to reassure her a bit as she helped me up the stairs and into our bedroom. With Paula's assistance, I managed to pull myself into the bed.

PJ jumped onto the bed with me, and after a couple of licks to my face, she became quiet as if she sensed something was wrong. She spent most of the day in my bed, her head resting on my lap as I stroked her ears. As the day wore on, Paula brought snacks hoping they would help me regain my strength.

In twenty-five years of marriage, Paula had only seen me sick a few times, and she had never seen me cry. She must have felt tremendous confusion and fear that afternoon to see me barely able to stand and sobbing so I could not speak. After a few moments, and between bursts of crying, I managed to say, "Mom told me that my brother used to beat me, and my dad didn't love me, not even a little." Paula could barely make sense of what I was saying, and I didn't have the energy to say more. Later, when I was able to explain to her exactly what happened, she was as shocked and confused by my mother's admission as I had been.

By late afternoon when I had gained some composure, I knew that I couldn't run a half-marathon. I was left with no energy nor desire to run Sunday's race. While I'd never dropped out of a race before, I couldn't imagine lacing up my running shoes. I called my running friends and told them I was sick and unable to run.

I never ran another race.

TRAIL OF OBSESSIONS

1976–1978
Southern Illinois

The summer of 1976 was a special time for my family and me. I had been teaching music at Southern Illinois University in Carbondale, Illinois, for five years after being discharged from the U.S. Navy Band. Paula and I had just celebrated our ninth wedding anniversary, and we had two wonderful daughters. We had developed friendships with several people in the area. We were ready to settle down. Some friends of ours had just built a home on the side of a hill with more space and less cost than buying an older home in town. We decided to do the same and build our dream home.

We purchased a one-and-a-half-acre site just six miles away from the university. The location was a heavily wooded area, minimally developed, and our home would be built near the top of a hill. We selected a two-story design with a walkout. The front was a combination of dark cedar siding and light-brown rock facing the street. The living room and master bedroom had large windows that looked down the hill. At the very edge of the property was an underground spring that fed into a nearby lake. This was going to be our final home, and all of us shared in the building of it. Even our daughters played an active role in planning their bedroom and the bathroom that would have twin sinks: no more putting up with your sister's toothpaste in your sink.

Building the house was a bit of an expense. Fortunately, my summer teaching schedule that year was light: a music appreciation class three mornings a week and morning trumpet lessons. This gave me time to do some of the physical work and lower the total cost of the house. I even enrolled in an electrical wiring class.

As with any major building project, challenges can be devastating or laughable. I had completed my wiring class and installed several outlets throughout the house. The main floor was an open concept with a large stone fireplace in the middle of a "great room" that ran the width of the house. I was feeling a bit cocky as I approached the more complex job of connecting two lamps to a single outlet above the fireplace mantel. Since the wires were long, I needed to cut and replace them with new cords leading from the lamps to the fireplace outlet. It was getting late, so I wanted to get the lamps wired before it got too dark to see. I'd called my wife and two daughters into the room to watch. They sat on three folding chairs facing the fireplace. I imagined my daughters admiring my wiring skills: "Our dad plays the trumpet, teaches music at the university, was in the Navy, and is now an electrician. Our dad is smart."

The sun had fallen behind the trees. In less than thirty minutes, it would be too dark to see. "Watch and learn," I told the ladies, "as I banish the darkness with light." I flourished my wire cutters for effect. I'd always had a flair for the dramatic.

I lifted the first wire with my left hand and let it dangle there. A phantom drumroll sounded in my mind, and then I cut it. Unfortunately, in my haste to impress "the ladies," I had forgotten to shut off the power. That's when the electricity surged through my body and tossed me across the floor like a bouncing ball. As soon as my wife and daughters realized that I was still breathing, we all had a good laugh. And just to play it safe, we agreed that my electrical wiring days were over.

We finished our new home in time to celebrate Thanksgiving. Life appeared to be going well for me. I was barely thirty, with a teaching position at a division one university. But by 1977, I began to lose interest in my job.

At that time, Southern Illinois University had massive budget problems, and faculty positions were being cut. In the music department, faculty began losing their interest in performing. Even the students sensed something was happening. Instead of hearing their professors practice in their studios, they saw us congregate in the faculty lounge, where each took turns sharing our unhappiness. We had forgotten that performing was the lifeblood of the music faculty. We went from a steady stream of performances to a limited few. When we did play a concert, the skill level was mediocre.

The reduced performances opened the door for anxiety. As a musician, I had never experienced this before. I began questioning my abilities as a performer. Performance anxiety led to a lack of musicality which fed my anxieties. Performing no longer calmed me and teaching no longer brought me joy.

During this time, I began talking with Ted and Lou, two friends who had made career moves from music to financial planning. They were selling insurance products, stocks, bonds, and financial services, making more money than I would ever make as a music teacher. They had spotted a business opportunity in nearby Effingham, a growing community with evidence of burgeoning incomes. It was a community in need of qualified financial planners. They invited me to join them. Meanwhile, the university continued to cut faculty positions. I worried if I didn't make a change soon, I would lose a job I wasn't even happy with.

When I held a family meeting and presented the prospect of moving to Effingham, I assumed my family would see this as a golden opportunity. Instead, my wife and daughters were shocked. They worried about leaving Carbondale. They fixated on the loss of friendships, current school, selling our dream home, and the fact that I would have to deal with a career change. I attempted to sell my family on the reasons this was a great idea, but Paula didn't see it. She also couldn't understand why I had not discussed this with her before bringing it to the whole family. "Where is this coming from?" she asked.

Instead of telling her about my anxiety and its impact on my performance, I focused on my loss of interest in teaching and the money that could be made in financial planning. But I began to feel uncomfortable over the decision. The family meeting ended with a collection of tears and anger all leveled at me. I've always believed that everyone usually makes one big mistake in their life, and I didn't want this to be the one for me.

I shared my situation with a few faculty members who were also unhappy with their job. They were much older than me, and they recommended I make the move. Expecting my current job to improve was unlikely. It could take years before it turned around. Meanwhile, Ted and Lou continued to focus on the business opportunities in the financial planning field.

I shared the recommendations of my faculty friends with Paula, and after a few weeks, she said she would support my decision to leave teaching and join Ted and Lou in Effingham. While she didn't want to move, she understood that I had a plan and was committed to seeing it through with me.

In June, I resigned from my faculty position and placed our home on the market.

Shortly after I signed the contract with Ted and Lou, Lou told me that he had been diagnosed with lung cancer. While he was feeling good, he assured me that I could cancel the contract if I preferred. He would understand. I don't remember if I ever considered it. If I didn't, I should have. The home we'd built together as a family still hadn't sold. Had I canceled the contract, I could have taken it off the market and kept my family in Carbondale. But I didn't. Lou said he was feeling great, so maybe he'd be fine. Terminating the contract felt like admitting to Lou that he was going to die. I felt it necessary to let him know that I believed in him. I did not feel it necessary to tell my wife that Lou had cancer and might die. I may have even put it out of my mind.

———

After we sold our home and purchased a house in Effingham, things began to fall apart. Lou's condition worsened. He had lost quite a bit of weight. His skin had turned a light yellow. At the same time, Ted had turned to religion, with the belief that he could lay hands on someone and heal them. I felt like I was in a situation where Lou was going to die, and Ted was going insane. Meanwhile, my wife was unhappy, and my daughters missed their friends.

A few weeks later, Ted and Marla, Lou's wife who shared Ted's belief in healing, asked me to meet them in the office. When I arrived, they thanked me for coming. They told me that Ted had laid his hands on Lou to heal him, yet Lou's condition was not improving. Ted suspected I didn't share the same beliefs in healing by the laying of hands. They believed that I was the weak link in the chain and that my disbelief was the reason Lou had not been healed. It was mandatory, they said, that I pray with Lou for his healing. I was surprised they wanted to pin Lou's lack of healing on me, but I wanted them to know I would do anything for Lou and wanted him to live. They said Lou was home resting and would be happy to see me.

I decided to do what they asked. I felt uncomfortable about it but rationalized that this was not about my feelings. This was about letting Lou know that I cared.

I followed Ted and Marla to her house. They ushered me into his bedroom. I told him I would like to pray for his healing. Lou said he was open to hearing my prayer and appreciated my efforts. I nodded. This was good, I thought. This was why I had come. I laid my hands on his head and said the prayer. I made certain I included the line, "I ask God and the Holy Spirit to heal you. In the name of God, the Holy Spirit, and the Holy Ghost."

Days later, Lou's health deteriorated, and he was hospitalized. In less than a week, Lou was dead. Ted blamed the hospital. He said they used the wrong medication or overmedicated him.

Paula and I agreed that I couldn't continue in this environment. The solution, we decided, would be to restore our life to what it was one year ago. I would return to a financial planning company in Carbondale, sell the Effingham house, find a temporary place to live in Carbondale until we could find a suitable house to buy, enroll the girls in their former school, and rejoin our friends.

I did everything I could to restore our life to the way it was and make my family happy again. Our Carbondale friends welcomed us back. When asked why I moved back so quickly, I said it was because one of my business associates died from lung cancer. But the truth was much worse. My decision to change careers was a huge mistake. It was selfish. It caused my family pain. Nothing good came of it. But worst of all, I had pressed forward in it despite the objections and pain it caused my family. This was not the husband or father I wanted to be. I hid the decision away and resolved to do better.

While the move to Effingham was the last time I disrupted my family's life to follow a passion, it wasn't the last time I switched from one obsession to another. This was a habit I had engaged in since the fourth grade when I became obsessed with playing the trumpet. When I look back at the passions I chased, they were like a series of shifting mirages. Each time one didn't deliver the fulfillment I looked for, I changed direction and chased the next one. In high school, I'd been president of my class and popular among my friends, but as soon as I graduated and went to college, my high school relationships ended. When I joined the U.S. Navy Band after college, I lost all contact with college friends, and upon my discharge from the Navy, my military friends were ignored. After five years of teaching music at Southern Illinois University, my musician friends were replaced with friends in the financial field, and I quit playing trumpet to concentrate on my new career. For ten years, I put all my energies into building my financial planning business.

By 1987, I was well-established in my career and didn't need to spend evenings and weekends at work. So I picked up racquetball and approached it with the same intensity I had approached music and business. I engaged in league play, tournaments, pickup games and purchased an expensive racquet, thinking it would add a few points to my game. I spent hours focusing on technique and reading books on the sport. When I started running to increase my physical stamina, the euphoria I experienced while floating down a country road as my feet barely touched the ground was remarkable. It was enough to stop playing racquetball and devote my time to running. Extended training led to longer runs and stronger highs. Each action became another obsession taken without consideration for my family and friends. At the time, I thought my passions made me happy, but any logical person might have said, "There's a problem in River City."

My wife, for whatever reason, didn't see the problem either. Paula supported each decision, no matter how surprising or disruptive. But I wouldn't understand how disruptive my shifting obsessions were until well into my fifties. Ironically, it would be that evening with my mother in October 1992 when she told me my brother Keith used to beat me, and my dad didn't love me even a little. That set me on a path to understanding who I was and why I felt the need to fill my life with one obsession after another.

STARVED FOR TRUTH

October 1992
Makanda, Illinois

Monday the 26th.

I awoke Monday morning with the sound of my alarm and got ready for work. The confusion from the weekend had not disappeared. I was determined to make it through the day. I focused on my morning appointments while storing my emotions in some imaginary mental compartment so others would not see. Between appointments, I kept my emotions from boiling up like day-old vomit. If I kept my office door closed and did not engage with co-workers, I would be okay. But as the day progressed, breathing required my attention. I needed help, but lessons from my childhood troubled me. *Deal with your own problems. Don't hang out your dirty laundry. Seeing a psychologist is a sign of weakness. Forget bad things, and they will go away.*

Normally I would have waited for my mind to bury whatever this was about, for my feelings of desperation to pass, and for my life to reboot. Then I thought of Dr. Martha Wright, a psychologist, and client who was also a good friend. Maybe she could help. I decided to give her a call.

She picked up after a few rings, and we engaged in small talk. My desperation must have seemed obvious because she asked me quickly, "Larry, what's bothering you?"

"Some things happened this weekend which I don't understand. I don't know where to begin. I think I might need your professional help."

She explained that since we were friends, a conflict of interest would prevent her from seeing me as a client. "But why don't you come over and tell me what happened?" she suggested. "Then, if you need, I could recommend someone for you to talk with." Her words made sense. I was certain that Martha could help me make sense of my confusion. We ended our conversation by agreeing to meet on Tuesday at 4:00 pm. *That sounded good*, I thought. *I can make it for another twenty-four hours. I'll just keep myself busy. I can do this.*

I spent the evening with my family watching television and eating popcorn. At one point, Paula asked how I was doing with all of this, and I told her I had an appointment with Martha the next day. "I just need to sort through some of this," I said. "It doesn't make any sense to me."

We both felt better knowing I was seeing a professional. Neither of us imagined this would be the next two decades of my life.

———

Tuesday the 27th.

I spent Tuesday as I had Monday, keeping my office door closed and not engaging with co-workers. I could breathe without a struggle, but I could not forget that my dad didn't love me, not even a little and that my brother beat me repeatedly with a hickory switch. I felt like the emotional grenade my mother had thrown had been embedded in my body and was about to explode. The push of a button or the pull of a wire and I would become a billion pieces of charred flesh and bones. The hours moved slower than anticipated. By the time I arrived at Dr. Wright's office, there was little doubt that I needed help.

The office was quiet with soft colors and comfortable furniture, and her Golden Retriever was there. The dog sat on the floor next to me. Petting her calmed my anxiety. I began to recount the conversation with my mother, explaining the shock and confusion of her words, how my reality had broken, and how I was questioning who I was.

"Larry, that must have been very upsetting for you. It sounds like someone dropped a bomb on your life."

"Yes, that's a good description. But I don't understand what it means or why I'm so upset."

"I think you need to talk with someone who will help you sort through all of this." I sat quietly while Martha considered the possibilities. "It's important to find the right match. Would you prefer talking with a man?"

My reaction was swift. "No, I don't want to talk with a man. I couldn't do that." My quick response surprised me, and I didn't know why. "I think I would feel more comfortable talking with a woman."

"Olivia, yes. Dr. Olivia Jennings is the one. She would be a perfect fit for you." Olivia was the director of the counseling center at Southern Illinois University and had been Martha's mentor while she completed the doctoral program.

"Let me call her and see if she is taking new clients."

After talking with Martha, my concerns about sharing information with a psychologist were dampened. I was relieved to hear that Dr. Jennings would see me Wednesday at 4:00 pm.

The next day was possibly the most important day of my life.

———

Wednesday the 28th.

I parked two blocks from Olivia's office. I stepped from my car, leaned my head downward and to the side, trying to blend into the landscape as I walked to her office. I entered the waiting room and buried my head into a magazine, hoping that I wouldn't see anyone I knew. Olivia Jennings arrived and introduced herself. The two of us entered her office.

The only furniture was a small loveseat, a chair, a side table with an accent lamp, and a box of tissues. This was not what I expected. Maybe I'd watched too many movies where the therapist's darkened office had a leather couch, overstuffed chair, and a large desk with a single lamp bent over an open file. The client would be stretched out on the couch while the therapist, with a yellow pad and fancy pen, worked her mental magic. Instead, I sat on the navy-blue loveseat while Olivia sat facing me in the matching chair. Next to the side table on my right was a small trash can overflowing with used tissues. I wondered what problems were discussed in this room.

"Larry, tell me why you wanted to see me."

"Well, I guess I should give you some background information. I have few memories of the first eight years of my life, which were spent on a farm with my mother, father, and a brother who was six years older than me. I just know that my parents divorced when I was almost eight, and I was sent away to live with my mother and grandparents in Louisville. As a child, I occasionally asked about my father. What was he like? What did he talk about? Did he have a sense of humor? I looked for any clue that might give me some information about my father. But each time I asked, my mother shared nothing. She just cried. I soon stopped asking. Last week all of that changed. She told me things that I never knew."

As I spoke, Olivia watched my every move. If I crossed my legs, rubbed my arm, talked fast or slow, or looked nervous, she noticed. I was there with a degree of apprehension, but her attention was not unsettling. She performed an emotional scan in the comfort of her office. That's how I felt.

Olivia continued to ask questions. "Tell me what your mother said."

I twisted in my seat, searching for the right words, the uncomfortable words. How I fell apart while driving home and how I'd never broken down in my entire life. After I recounted the story as best I could, Olivia leaned forward and held my hand. Looking back, I realize I never said anything about my brother.

"Larry, you've experienced the resurfacing of some traumatic memories which were triggered by comments that your mother made. At the moment, things might seem confusing. But in time, it will begin to make sense." She paused. "I promise that everything will be okay and that I'll be here to support you. I would like for you to come back next week at the same time. Meanwhile, keep a written journal of your thoughts for the week."

There is something, perhaps unexplainable, that happens between a client and a therapist when they are a good match. I felt good about my first session with Olivia. I was surprised by her empathy for my situation. This was probably the first time I had ever talked with someone who appeared to be so concerned about my well-being. It was a special feeling.

That night, after dinner, I went right to bed. Normally I might have finished some work I'd brought home from the office or spent the evening watching some television with the family, but I was exhausted and needed to sleep. I looked forward to going to bed and turning the lights off. I could only hope that tomorrow would be a better day.

Sometime in the middle of the night, I had a dream filled with detailed images and sexual suggestions accompanied by an erection. It was like a mental video showing two people having sexual intercourse. But this was different. It was a penis moving in and out of something void of pubic hair. I woke, confused and dismayed by what I had seen. Olivia had instructed me to maintain a journal of my feelings, but there was no way I could tell her about this. Who knows what she would make of it? I spent the rest of the night drifting in and out of sleep, wondering why I would have had such a dream and what it could mean.

————

Thursday the 29th.

I woke on Thursday feeling better than I had in days. I felt normal. My wife and I had made plans for a weekend trip to visit our oldest daughter and her family in Wisconsin. I began looking forward to the trip with the same anticipation I had felt before the night my life unraveled in my mother's living room.

At work, I kept my office door open and interacted with co-workers. Nothing unusual happened. There was no turmoil, no confusion, leaving me to wonder if maybe I didn't need to see a psychologist.

That evening I relaxed, watched some television, and retired around 10:30 pm. Well into the night, I returned to the dream I had experienced the night before: a penis was moving in and out of something devoid of pubic hair. But unlike before, this dream took on a whole new dimension. It was accompanied by the sensation of my anus in an open position. I suddenly woke up. *It's my brother, Keith. Oh my God, it's Keith.*

While my body was covered in sweat, I was cold and unable to stand. I slid out of bed onto the floor, turned, and grabbed hold of the mattress while I rolled back and forth, hyperventilating. I crawled to the bathroom and hugged the stool, feeling my body expel what seemed like poison. Dry heaves followed; strains of saliva dripped into a pool of colored water. I rested my head on the toilet seat. Trying to make sense of the moment, I was met with no answers except for one. *Keith had raped me.*

Not knowing what to expect if I went back to bed, I lay on the tiled bathroom floor with my arms wrapped around the stool. If I fell asleep, was there more to come? Minutes, hours passed while I hesitated, uncertain. Eventually, I returned to my bed and waited for morning.

————

Friday the 30th.

The next morning, I left for work at 6:30 am – more than an hour earlier than I normally would. I wanted to get to work before anyone else. I needed to call Olivia, but it had to be a private call. I hoped she would be in. As soon as the clock reached 8:00 am, I made the call. One ring, two rings, someone answered and transferred my call to Olivia. Thank God.

I told Olivia about my dream and how upsetting it was, and how I lost control of myself. I explained how Paula and I had planned on traveling to Wisconsin to visit our daughter and her family for the weekend. But I didn't know what might surface in my brain and if it was safe for me to leave town. I asked her what I should do.

She told me to go ahead and make the trip. She said it would be good for me to get away and enjoy the company of family. She advised me not to think about dreams. "You've buried memories for more than forty years," she said. "A few more days shouldn't make a difference. When you return, we will discuss it in the safety of my office." Her compassion and concern were unlike anything I had felt before. While it was an unfamiliar feeling, it was good.

I took her advice and made the trip as planned, concentrating on the time with my family and visiting my favorite bookstores. If a hint of something uncomfortable began to appear, I directed it to a mental compartment in my brain, stored away for another day.

Paula and I left our daughter's home on Sunday morning. Four hours into the seven hour drive back, we passed by the Farmer City Road exit. Ten miles down that road was the farmhouse my family and I had lived in until I was seven. For years, every time we returned from a visit with my daughter and her family, I had considered taking the exit.

"Someday, I have to take a trip to the farm," I said to my wife.

"You talk about that quite a bit. Why is that?"

"Well, it's where I lived for the first seven years of my life. I'm always thinking about the place, and now I'm wondering if a visit would help me remember what it was like. I keep wondering if what my mother said is accurate."

"How would you feel about planning another trip to Wisconsin in a couple of weeks? We could leave a little earlier and make time to visit the farm. We'll be within ten miles of it."

"I'm okay with that," I said.

"Okay, let's do it. I'm curious to see the place myself."

Six years later, we visited the farm.

Trust Is a Miracle

November 1992
Southern Illinois

Tuesday was my appointment with Olivia. As she led me into her office, I noticed that the trash can next to the loveseat, which had been full of used tissues at my last visit, was nearly empty. I wondered if I was her only patient that day or if her previous sessions had been mild. Over the next decade, I would look into that trash can at the beginning of every session and use it as a barometer of what kind of day Olivia was having. An empty can meant light conversation; a full can meant she'd had a heavy day.

"How are you feeling? How was your trip to Wisconsin?"

"I feel good. I must have sounded awful when I called you last Friday. But now everything is okay."

"That's good. I'm glad you're feeling better. Tell me about the dream you experienced."

As I described the dream, trying to visualize the whole thing in my mind, the nausea returned, and the muscles in my stomach cramped. Olivia pushed the trash can next to me.

"Go ahead and use it if you need to. You can do anything in front of me. This is your safe place."

I began to shake and dry heave into the can. Saliva dripped in messy threads from my mouth. When my stomach stopped cramping, I used the tissues to wipe my mouth as best I could and then leaned back into the loveseat. I was shaky, and my skin felt cold. This was not at all what I had expected.

I had begun therapy, intending to discover my true reality, not some made-up narrative of wishful thinking. I had no idea the process would affect me this viscerally. If I was dry-heaving into a wastebasket on day two, how much worse was it going to get? Olivia told me that therapy would be long and challenging, that I would not be the same afterward. I would be able to soar. "You have some terrible memories that need to be addressed," Olivia told me. "We'll move slowly. Too many memories at one time could be overwhelming, making it difficult to perform your day-to-day tasks. Imagine taking an onion and gradually peeling away one layer at a time. That's what we'll do. We will work on the difficult parts when you're in the safety of my office, making certain you're put back together and feeling better before you leave. Are you prepared to do that, Larry? Will you trust me?"

Her words sounded flat to me. I was not used to trusting, and I could not imagine what lay ahead. But desperation gave me the courage to move forward, a willingness to look into the abyss.

"Yes, Olivia. I can do this."

One of the first questions Olivia asked me was if I had ever engaged in suicide ideation. I said no. I would never commit suicide. This was a lie. Thoughts of suicide had served me well my entire life, much like a child's security blanket. My plan was simple and painless. I would sit in my car while parked in a closed garage, connect a hose from inside the car to the exhaust pipe, play soothing music on the radio, take some sleeping pills, and drink a bottle of wine. This was my teenage plan. I held a similar plan when I was older. Suicide was my ace-in-the-hole, a guarantee that I would keep a measure of control in my life. I could not imagine relinquishing it as an option. But if I told Olivia the truth, I would be admitted to a mental hospital for observation. So I lied.

It didn't occur to me at the time that my lie had immediately violated the trust Olivia promised me. But for me, trust, the centerpiece of therapy, was unfamiliar, even elusive. How could I let go of my built-up defenses and open myself to the unknown, even if it was the path to healing?

Though I wasn't prepared to trust Olivia, I was committed to the therapeutic process. She cautioned me to be careful with who I entrusted my story. "Pick your friends wisely. Protect your fragile state. Each day you will become stronger and wiser, but it will take time before you can soar." Other ground rules she established were, "Don't jump to conclusions. Don't force memories to surface. Build a support group. Don't read books about sexually abused children for six months. We will not use hypnosis. We will use meditation for relaxation and for breaking down walls that may be hiding memories. The strategy is to retrieve, not to construct. We'll use memories that you haven't buried to survey your unconscious and describe your past and present behaviors."

I challenged Olivia on this one. "How can the past I haven't forgotten help me know if what my mother said is true? Isn't the whole point that my mind has hidden the abuse from me?"

Olivia held my gaze for a moment, then she said, "Larry. Even if the abuses your brother subjected to your six-year-old body didn't leave memories, they left tracks."

EVERYTHING BURIED
BUT NOTHING GREW

1993
Olivia's office

During the early part of my therapy, Olivia and I engaged in sessions where we discussed the need to examine my past and present behaviors. I often found myself in an emotional wilderness, a human desert where everything was buried, but nothing grew. Examining my actions provided the opportunity to understand myself and to improve the quality of my life. The beauty of our discussions was that Olivia pointed me down paths I wouldn't have seen, leaving the traversing part to me.

I remember one session which focused on why I was uncomfortable with men. While a one-to-one ratio was doable, hanging out with a group of men was uncomfortable.

"Can you give me some examples when you felt uncomfortable with men?"

I told her about a time when I was thirteen. My mother decided that I should attend a summer church camp for boys. Since church was important to my mother, she must have thought spending a week with boys in a church environment would be good for me.

"Was it?" Olivia asked.

"Definitely not. The camp turned out to be a horrible experience. Sleeping in the dormitory with several boys felt so threatening that I barely made it through the night. I was nervous and felt unsafe and imagined that something bad was about to happen. I just didn't know what. I called my mother the next day and told her that I was sick, had a sore throat, and needed to come home. Since my home was only a seven-minute drive away, I knew she could pick me up if she wanted to. I milked the story so much that my mother began to believe that I was really sick and needed to come home. After several phone calls and more stories of my misery, she picked me up on the third day."

"What did she say?"

"Nothing. She thought I was really sick. I put on a good show for her, and I went right to bed when she took me home."

"Did she send you back next year?"

"No. I suppose she might have, but I was selected for another camp."

"Tell me about it," Olivia said.

I looked up. As always, Olivia was watching me carefully. I forced a laugh. "Well, there was a local Lions Club in my hometown that sent two boys each year to a summer camp. It was an all-expenses-paid trip for boys in need, and I was chosen. I objected, but my mother told me what an honor it was.

"'You'll love it,' my mother said. 'I know you didn't like the church camp, but that was because you were sick. This will be different. And how could you tell them you don't want to go? That would be unforgivable.'

"She went on and on. You know, typical mother guilt and shame. I finally agreed to go, and even though I didn't understand why, I still hated it, just like before. But I managed to stay the entire week. After all, the camp was over a hundred miles away. I had no choice but to stay and pretend I was having a good time. When we returned from the trip, we were required to give a short talk to the Lions Club on the experience. In my speech, I thanked them for sending me. I told them what a wonderful experience the camp was. All lies."

"Let's talk about the anxiety you experienced while at the summer camps. Do you have other negative experiences with men?"

It didn't take me long to come up with another example. "Oh yes, I remember it well. It was June of 1967 when I enlisted in the U.S. Navy. Before my transfer to the band, I was obligated to complete eleven weeks of basic training in Chicago."

"Tell me about the experience."

"It was horrible. I knew it was going to be difficult, but I didn't know why."

"Was boot camp worse than your camp experiences as a teenager?"

"Yes, it was worse. Talking about it makes me nervous."

"Was your anxiety due to the physical training you experienced?"

"No, not at all. It was an emotional experience. I can give you an example." I hesitated.

"Go ahead."

"When I walked through the front door, the recruits were dressed in different clothing and haircuts. All appeared to have individual identities. I joined a line of several recruits waiting to have their heads shaved. We then undressed and gave them our civilian clothing in exchange for military clothes. When we walked out the back door, we all looked the same. It was difficult to tell one recruit from the other."

"Did you feel like you were losing your identity?"

"Oh yes. I looked like a different person and felt like a different person. The next morning, we lined up for breakfast. Long lines were common in boot camp. As we waited in line, one of the officers was yelling something. Since I couldn't make out what he was saying, I asked the recruit behind me what the officer was yelling.

"'Nuts to butts,' the recruit said. I couldn't believe it. I thought I must have misheard him.

"'Nuts to butts? Is that what you just said?' He nodded. In other words, we were to move closer to the recruit standing in front of us.

"That's all I needed to hear. I'm supposed to press my penis against the recruit's butt? What a repulsive introduction to boot camp. I get sick to my stomach just thinking about it."

"Why do you think it was so difficult for you?"

"Well, I can see a connection between my experiences at the church camps, the eleven-week boot camp, and the physical and sexual abuse I experienced as a child. I suppose I was afraid that I might be subjected to sexual abuse. The group showers didn't help. Neither did the double rows of stools where everyone faced each other."

"So, Larry, what does that tell you?"

"Each time I find myself in a similar situation, I become very anxious. I fear for my safety. I can see the childhood physical and sexual abuse written all over it. At boot camp, I tried to resist going to the restroom for a bowel movement. I waited until lights out when most of the recruits were asleep. Then I slipped into the restroom to take care of business. Occasionally there would be a couple of recruits present. We all tried not to look at each other."

"Oh my. That must have been awful for you."

"It was. Now I wonder about those other recruits. I imagine I wasn't the only one there who was dealing with uncomfortable emotions."

Olivia nodded. "I'm sure you weren't. Now that we know what caused the uncomfortable emotions, we can better deal with the causes. It will require sitting with the memories to reduce your pain. While it might seem difficult, you can do this. Now, before you go, I want you to visualize a safe place and feel the peace."

I began to meditate while Olivia held my hand. "Larry, we made progress today. You're doing good work."

When I would return home in the evening after my appointments, I enjoyed downtime with the family. I'd ask the girls about school, homework, and the latest gossip and ask Paula about her day teaching second graders at Unity Point School and what we would do on Saturday night. You might wonder what I contributed to the evening conversations. The answer is very little. I didn't tell them about my latest session with Olivia when my body was shaking, and my arms were wrapped around her trash can. These weren't acceptable discussions at the evening meal. Paula knew my life was consumed by memories, dreams, nightmares, visualizations, and that was enough.

When the evening surrendered to darkness and my family went to bed, I went downstairs to the lower floor of our bi-level house—my cave. This was where I worked on my blueprint for recovery using a combination of meditation and visualization. The meditation relaxed my mind, making it more receptive. The visualization, which is more active, pushed my mind in a specific direction. Together, I recalled the floor plan of the farmhouse and barn in De Land, Illinois.

I would sit in an easy chair and cross my legs in a yoga-like position. I then turned off the lamp next to my chair. Except for the glow from a nightlight plugged into the outlet next to the chair, the room was dark. I believe this sliver of light was more conducive to the healing process. Establishing a level of comfort was important.

I began by listening to each breath as I inhaled and then exhaled. The objective was to relax and feel myself move into a quiet environment with no distraction. In time, the relaxation from meditation became easier and longer. I began with a mere minute or two followed by fifteen to thirty minutes, and eventually one hour. With increased periods of meditation came a state of euphoria similar to what I had felt with running. It was like the emotional bliss I felt as a musician when playing a lyrical phrase and experiencing the tension and release found in the final cadence.

Once I was fully relaxed through meditation, I used visualization to peer into other areas of my brain. I focused on the barn, the house, and our family when we were a family. I then imagined a floor plan of the house and barn. I felt like I was looking down into a dollhouse with no roof. In the beginning, the images were blurry but cleared up as I focused. In time they became crystal clear. The repressed memories were always connected to stories that were violent and sexual.

Each week I shared everything with Olivia: dreams, memories, visualizations, meditations, everything that happened throughout the week. Olivia performed an analysis by studying my emotional reactions to the stories. Was I calm, anxious, out-of-sorts, confused, or in need of the trash can? She was always able to show me the way without telling me the way. I always went back to my cave to learn more about the farmhouse until everything was clear: the living room sofa and chairs covered with sheets, the wood-burning stove in the kitchen, the sink with a hand pump connected to an outside well, the bedroom on the main floor, and another in an open stairwell leading to the upstairs where all the rooms were unused. The memories of the barn were especially vivid.

THE FARM

1948
De Land, Illinois

Six years old.

As a child, I often looked out the hayloft to see an endless sea of corn, soybeans, and wheat. A southwesterly wind stirred ripples across the landscape; tractors and farm machinery moved slowly, and from a distance, farmhouses, barns, and machine sheds seemed no bigger than Monopoly pieces.

We lived in a big, two-story house sitting on nearly five hundred acres of rich Illinois farmland. In exchange for working the land, Robert Engel, who reportedly owned more than four thousand acres, paid my dad a modest salary and let us live in the house, a house we pretended to own. My dad's brother, James, had a similar arrangement with Mr. Engel. Their house was no more than a mile north of us. His sons, John and Sammy, spent a considerable amount of time at our house.

My world extended a mile-and-a-half south to De Land, a small town with a diner, a schoolhouse, summer outdoor movies, a general store, and a church where my mother went when things got bad.

My father taught me how to keep my hoe sharp when cutting corn stalks out of bean rows and how to use the weight of my body to swing the hoe like a pendulum. My mother taught me how to milk a cow the right way: no yanking or pulling, just a gentle massage where my hands created a rhythm, first left, then right, over and over again. But no one told me why the sun came up in the morning and settled down at night; how a catfish can swim underwater and never take a breath; why Keith went to the grove of hickory trees, cut a three-foot switch, and came looking for me. I remember the switch striking my body and the burning sensation that followed. One blow and another, and the blood soon appeared. When boredom moved in, Keith turned and walked away.

Keith must have talked to me, but I don't recall him speaking a single word. But I do remember how he floated ghostlike across the ground as if he had no legs, and his breath on the back of my neck was hot. Keith's head turned left, right, and sometimes spun around in a continuous circle. He was too mean to be real.

John and Sammy often came to our house looking for ways to pass the day. As the youngest, I tagged along, hoping for the slightest bit of attention. Keith sometimes handed out hickory switches to the cousins. The three of them formed a circle, with me standing in the center. The object of the game was to hit me with the switches and not allow me to break the circle. If I ran in one direction, that boy would drive me back to the middle, where they hit me until I fell to the ground and assumed a fetal position.

Imagine a dog that has been severely beaten by its owner. The look in the dog's eyes reflects a bone-hard sadness; his back is arched; his rib cage looks like the bars on a jail cell. If you were to kick him, he likely would remain curled up on the ground. Like the dog, I always chose flight over fight. If I didn't fight back, they sometimes became bored and walked away.

Sometimes my mother showed my dad the marks on my body, but he just turned and walked away. I often wonder why he didn't stop Keith and my cousins. Did he care? Did he think that the beatings were needed to turn a boy into a man? Maybe that's what he thought.

When the pain was severe, I escaped to the cornfields where the stalks stood straight and bent slightly against a stiff wind. There was a measure of safety as my dog and I hid within the green foliage. Even today, I still cherish the beauty of a mature cornfield, the wall of safety, and a bit of stale air as dragonflies zoom over a puddle of water. As an adult, I once took my new camera into a fully-grown cornfield and photographed its natural beauty. I enjoyed getting on the ground and focusing on the rows of corn stalks. At the time, I didn't understand the significance of the cornfields. I just knew they were beautiful.

One day, my family was having a typical farmer's breakfast: bacon, eggs, fried potatoes, and a bowl of chalk-white gravy with sprinkles of bacon floating about. No one ever talked at breakfast, but this morning was more tense than usual. Dad told Keith that he could not go with him to the fields and would have to stay at the house. Keith's eyes turned a fiery red. I looked down at my plate, hoping he did not notice me. As Dad finished his breakfast and headed out the door, I stuck to his side until we walked onto the porch. I raced for the cornfield and found a good spot where I could see the house and still have plenty of room for my escape. Keith stepped onto the front porch and looked to the left, to the right, and toward the cornfield. I worked my way through the maze of corn stalks and slipped around the base of each stalk like a giant snake until I found a barren spot where my dog and I sat for hours.

A few years after my father and mother had divorced, one of the cousins, Sammy, told me about a time when my mother scared me so much that I stopped spending the day in the cornfield. One day, so the story goes, my mother wanted to stop me from hiding in the cornfield. She watched, and when she saw me go into the cornfield, she dressed in a scary costume that would frighten any five-year-old boy. She ran parallel to the cornfield and waited for me to appear. When I reached the end of the field, my mother was waiting. Her costume was so scary that I raced back to the house. She was waiting at the house for me as if nothing had happened. I told her about the monster I saw. She suggested that I never run to the cornfield again. She didn't realize or didn't care that the cornfield was my only safe place.

On this particular day, hours later, as I had done many times before, I moved to the edge of the field, hesitated, then walked toward the house, turned, and looked in all directions. Except for the distant sound of my dad's tractor, it was quiet. Each board creaked as I moved up the porch stairs into the house. I yelled for my mother, but no response. I sat in a rocker in front of a window that faced the barn some two hundred yards from the window. I don't know how long I was sitting there before I saw my mother bolt from the barn, followed by Keith, who swung a hickory switch in the air. Her screams bounced off one building and then another as she neared the house. She ran up the front steps, through the kitchen door, and across the living room floor toward the stairs to the second floor. Fear was in her eyes.

Keith chased her up the stairs to the second floor. There was the sound of running feet and then a thud as something hit the floor. My body shook. I gathered the courage to carefully slip up the stairs toward the bedroom on the second floor. The room no one slept in. Peering around the corner, I saw my brother on top of my mother. My mother and I never talked about that day.

ANOTHER KIND OF DISEASE

December 1992
Makanda, Illinois

Sometimes I think it would have been easier if I'd had cancer or another more socially acceptable disease. The physician would have shown my family an X-ray of my tumor and prescribed a course of treatment, giving them hope that they could openly share with their friends. Or maybe it would have been better if my wife had taken me to a hospital and said, "Something is wrong with my husband. He is depressed and having nightmares. He's downright miserable."

After performing a CT scan, the doctor might have said, "We've determined your husband's problem. As you can see from the images, his soul is being strangled by massive adhesions. The different-colored adhesions represent a specific type of abuse, with the number of strains revealing the frequency. Look here, and you can see how the CT scan tells a story. The blue striations tell us your husband was sexually molested by his older brother. Based on the massive number of strains, we estimate his brother's penis was rammed up his anus more than one thousand times."

"Can anything be done to help him?"

"Oh, yes. He can be treated with medications and work with a psychologist who will help loosen the grip of the adhesions and terminate their growth. They can never be removed, but he can recover. However, he will likely become a different person from the one you know."

"What if we don't do anything?"

"Well, that's an option," the doctor might have said. "However, if you choose that option, you might as well cut a hole in his side, tie a rope around his neck, and hang him from a tree. It's more humane. And untreated abuse victims make the best birdhouses."

———

My mother and I traveled down Interstate 57 to Makanda. It had been our tradition that my mother join my family for the Christmas holidays. We talked about the forecast for light to medium snow and how cold this winter was. It had been two months after my mother's revelations, and I was six weeks into psychotherapy. Memories had begun to surface, and my mental health was challenged. Fragments of history, a piece here or there, and sometimes a complete story surfaced. But they were just memories. And how could I be sure they were true?

My mother probably had a wealth of information that could help me work through my struggles. Perhaps a moving car with nowhere to escape could be a good place to ask her questions.

"Ever since you told me about Keith beating me, I've had nightmares. A psychologist is helping me sort through all of this stuff. But I could use your help."

Startled, she looked my way. "Well, why on earth would you need a psychologist?" she said with a huff. "Why would you want to bring up bad things in your past?"

The answer seemed obvious: I needed to know my history to regain my sanity. "I just want to know. Some of my nightmares have been about Keith doing sexual things to me. Did you see Keith do anything to me?" There was a desperate tone in my voice.

She stared forward. "Well, I can't imagine that happening. But I wouldn't have any way of knowing about that." She paused. "Oh, I suppose it's possible something could have happened."

"What do you mean? You were there. What did you see?"

"I didn't see anything. I was busy doing my chores. I wouldn't have known what was going on in the barn."

The barn, I thought. That's where Keith had raped me. She knew what had happened. "So, you're telling me you didn't know that Keith did stuff to me in the barn?"

"No," she snapped. "I don't know anything about that, and I'm not going to sit around and try to remember the past."

"So what should I do? Just forget about it, and it will go away?"

"Yes, that's right. If you don't think about the past, after a while, it just goes away. I'll tell you right now, I'm not going to think about that stuff."

I shouldn't have been surprised by my mother's thinking. While she had several friends connected to the church and a positive relationship with her grand-children, that didn't carry over to our relationship. My role was to keep my distance and not upset her. It was a superficial relationship at best.

My life was equally vapid. I had developed a routine where I pigeonholed each aspect of my life into a sepa-rate pocket, providing the illusion that I was in control. I always had plans for this or that or whatever. The finan-cial planning practice was kept in one pocket, hobbies in another, family life in another, and so on. But when the repressed memories began to surface, my artificial walls began to crumble. I couldn't be the dutiful son she wanted. I demanded answers to questions she refused to consider. Our relationship became cold and bitter.

Three days later, my mother and I were traveling up Interstate 57 to take her home. She had spent a pleas-ant if pedantic Christmas with her granddaughters. The weather was cold, and the mood in the car was raw. There were no questions this time, just small talk to push the passage of time. I felt lonely that day. Olivia had warned me of this. Life will never be the same, is what she'd said. I wonder now if I had wanted a different relationship with my mother, but how does one have a loving rela-tionship with someone who is unable to feel?

PART II
THE INCONCEIVABLES

MEMORIES CONFIRMED

June 10, 1998
De Land, Illinois

For six years, I spent my evenings meditating in the lower level of our home, building the blueprint for my recovery while struggling with the validity of my memories. What I dug up at times seemed so outlandish that I questioned my sanity. My mother would not share any additional information; my brother and father were dead, and the two cousins who had accompanied Keith and me to the barn were not approachable.

One night, after I'd retreated to the lower level of my house, I turned the lights down and sat with my legs folded in my favorite chair. My body seemed to float throughout the room. Uninvited words, sentences, and phrases poured into my mind. The structure and rhymes were like poetry. The fact that I had never written poetry before made this revelation more striking. My only writing consisted of the occasional letter to a client or a brief note to a friend. I awoke from a trance, a mental space I had never visited before. *Could this be poetry, and if so, could I write it on paper?*

I walked away from the chair to my computer ten feet away. I placed my hands on the keyboard and took a deep breath. I began to type rapidly, without attention to individual words. Minutes later, my fingers stopped. There, on the computer screen, was a compelling poem I could not ignore. It felt like a miracle. While the poem was crude and unrefined, it was powerful. Most importantly, it included details of what had been done to me in the barn, details which left little doubt that my brother Keith had raped me.

I shared my poem with Olivia, who encouraged me to continue writing. It provided a creative way of accessing memories that had, up to that point, visited me only in the form of nightmares.

As I continued the therapy sessions with Olivia, my support circle expanded. Because meditation had become a staple in my spiritual growth after therapy, I began studying with Charlotte McCloud, a local yoga and meditation teacher. Each session ended with Charlotte emptying a backpack full of books onto the padded floor. The students then circled her, hoping to pick up some additional information and rest in the aura of Charlotte's quiet ways. When I told her about the conversation with my mother and how she told me that my father didn't love me, not even a little, her response was quick and to the point. "Tell your mother to go to hell."

One day in the spring of 1998, Paula asked me how my blueprint for recovery was going. She knew I was using meditation and visualization as tools to discover the layout of the farmhouse and barn in De Land. She knew I wanted to test my memories against the truth. In the beginning, we hadn't discussed my therapy much, but over the past six years, we'd talked a lot about it during those seven-and-a-half drives to Wisconsin. She knew how important a trip to the farm was for me, and perhaps she wanted to hold me accountable for doing it.

"While I have so many memories of the farm," I said, "I admit to being a little afraid to walk up to the front door and ask if I can see the inside of their house. How will they react to my sudden appearance? Will they allow me to look around?"

"They can either say yes or no. What do you have to lose? And I'll be with you for support. You need to do this."

I knew she was right. We were making a trip to Wisconsin in two weeks, and it was decided we would visit the farm on our way back. It would be June 10th, our thirtieth wedding anniversary.

I rehearsed my trip to the farm and what I would say. We decided not to tell our daughter of our intentions for the trip back. She knew about my past and the fact that I was in therapy, but Paula and I didn't know what might happen with the visit. If the farm's layout matched the blueprint from my meditations, I would know my memories were true. On the other hand, if they didn't match, it could be devastating. I wanted to keep the visit private.

Paula and I had a lovely visit with our daughter and her family. We left early Wednesday morning, and by noon we were driving down the Farmer City Road exit. In ten miles, I would be at the farmhouse my family and I had lived in until I was seven.

Illinois winters are long and cold, but when spring comes, and the land thaws, the earth comes alive. Central Illinois didn't make the Seven Wonders of the World list but don't tell that to an Illinois farmer who calls a handful of dirt "black gold." To walk barefoot across a field and feel the warm soil push up between your toes, or to hear corn grow during the night, is spiritual for those who believe.

A few miles from the farmhouse, I slowed the car and rolled down the windows. The temperature was 70 degrees with a slight southwesterly breeze coming in at 10 miles per hour. The countryside was just as I remembered: beans thick and heavy from the morning dew and cornstalks that stood straight like soldiers. I imagined the farmer who had driven into that field pulling a four-bottom plow. I imagined the steel blades cutting into the rich, black soil that had just the right amount of moisture—not so wet as to be like mud or so dry as to be like cement. I saw the soil turning and churning behind him like freshly kneaded bread, worms waking from their long winter's nap, and robins flying down from the sky, looking to be fed. The farmer, the father I'd imagined I'd had, would have breathed in the scent of spring— freshly turned soil mixed with gasoline fumes—as the tractor moved through the earth, exhaling puffs of smoke. Life would have been pretty much near perfect. There'd been a time, living in the white weathered farmhouse just down the road, when I thought I wanted to be that man. As I gazed out the window, a smile crossed my face. It was a beautiful day to search the archives in my mind.

We arrived. Except for a new tin roof, the red barn looked the same. The machine shed, its boards faded a light gray, looked older than I remembered. The outhouse was missing, but I wasn't surprised. To the left was the familiar grove of hickory trees with trunks that had grown to the size of a large man's waist. To the right, and at the end of the sidewalk, was the two-story house that didn't flinch when I looked its way. Up the steps leading to the front porch was one door when I remembered two. For some reason, I wasn't alarmed by this. I just assumed the new owners had done some remodeling. It had been a long time since I'd been there.

I parked the car and walked up to the house with Paula. Two knocks, then three, and a middle-aged woman pushed the screen door slightly ajar. I was apprehensive, a little anxious, but I was ready to do this. After all, I had spent years preparing.

"I used to live here some forty-five years ago and just happened to be in the area. Would it be possible for me to look around?" The part about me just being in the area was false but made a better story than the truth: "Hi. I've planned this visit for the past six years, and I just want to compare the layout of your house to the blueprint in my mind to know if my brother really raped me. Mind if I come in?" No. The lie was more comfortable than the truth.

"Yes," the woman answered. "That would be fine. But the house is a mess. I need a few minutes to pick things up. You can look around outside, and that will give me a chance to make the house presentable."

"Sure. Thank you!" I felt the joy and satisfaction that I was going to see the inside of my first home and gratitude that this woman was willing to let us in.

As Paula and I left the porch and waited in the front yard, she expressed the same shock that I felt. "I can't believe the lady is going to let us look around in her house. And she doesn't even know who we are!"

I agreed. "Yes, it's amazing. She seems very nice." I knew there was no way Paula would have done the same in the woman's situation.

Even though we had discussed this visit for years in those car rides from Wisconsin, it felt unbelievable to be let in. And the woman was even tidying up the house for us. It was incredible. I knew I wanted to ask her about the entrance to the house—why there was only one door instead of two—but it wasn't the only thing on my mind. There was so much else to see.

While we waited, we scanned the landscape. For me, every angle, every view evoked a memory.

I pointed out a spot one hundred yards from the house in the direction of the barn: "There's where the outhouse stood—spiders in the summer, freezing temperatures in the winters, not a place to sit and think. 'Do it quickly' is what my dad said." I told Paula about when my dad and Uncle James made me and Sammy, who was barely nine, clean the outhouse. My father pushed the outhouse on its side, exposing a three-by-five-foot hole dug to a depth of two and a half feet. He then instructed us to scoop the shit into a bucket and dump it into a manure spreader, where it would become fertilizer for a nearby field. I was seven and didn't have the strength to lift a full five-gallon bucket, let alone one loaded with human waste, so I had to take one-half bucket at a time.

Some fifty feet in front of the house was the well we had used decades ago. A hand pump was attached to the kitchen sink, which delivered an endless supply of cool water even on the hottest days. After heating buckets of water on top of an old, steel-gray wood stove, my mother emptied one bucket at a time into a galvanized tub, raising the water temperature to just the right level for our weekly baths.

Paula could hardly believe it. "Oh my God, Larry! This reminds me of *Little House on the Prairie.* I'm seeing a side of you I've never seen before. Having an outhouse, no running water, or a water heater is primitive."

"Well, your dad was a dentist. Mine was a farmer."

Just then, the screen door swung open, and we returned to the front porch. We were about to enter the place where I had spent the first seven years of my life. Things were falling in place so easily, I wondered if God or some other force was playing a role in my recovery.

The woman stepped out to join us. "I forgot to introduce myself," she said. "My name is Jean Borders, and I live here with my husband and two children. Both of our children are students at the University of Illinois."

"That's where I went to school," I said. "Graduated in 1967. My name is Larry Franklin, and this is my wife, Paula." I felt an immediate bond with Jean as we stood on the front porch and talked about how much the campus had changed, where her children lived, and where I had lived while on campus.

When she invited us into the house, I pointed to the single entrance and asked her, "Didn't there used to be two doors leading off the front porch?"

Jean looked a bit startled. "Why yes, the outside door leading to the kitchen was closed years ago." That made me feel good.

Jean ushered us into the family room, which had a large cased opening leading to the kitchen. "Didn't there used to be a single door to the kitchen?" I asked. "I don't remember the large opening."

"You're right," Jean answered. "Several years ago, we decided to open things up. Removing the door and opening the wall seemed to be a good idea."

The structural changes gave the house a more modern appearance. In the past, each room had resembled an individual box, sealed off by doors, making it easier to heat a particular room during the winter. There was no central heating in those days.

"It certainly opened things up," I said, walking across the room. "I remember a kerosene stove that stood in this corner. It was vented through the wall and into the flue that was connected to the living-room fireplace." Jean nodded. "That was before we moved in. We've lived here twenty-three years, and my husband's parents were here before us."

As Jean talked, my thoughts reached back to when a host of stories had browbeaten this house. A time when I imagined the walls moved slightly in and out, and a raspy, high-pitched sucking sound was accompanied by the low drumming of a heartbeat—*ra-dommm, ra-dommm, ra-dommm.*

My childhood family moved with me from one room to the next. Keith sat in a corner looking through a stack of comic books. My mother sat at her sewing machine making me a shirt from a recently emptied chicken feed sack, and my dad walked through dressed in his usual attire: white T-shirt and work pants.

We walked into the main bedroom, where Keith and Dad slept together in a double bed. I felt uneasy and moved closer to Paula. My mother had told me that Keith and Dad began sleeping together when I was four. That it was to protect me from the bad things my brother did. "It was your dad's idea," my mother had repeated over and over. Even in summer, this room was always cold. Standing in that room, I recalled a memory that I had pushed away for years, and I pushed it away again. It was better forgotten.

Jean led us to the kitchen. My family sat at the table. Except for the occasional slurp, a metal fork scraping the last morsel of food from a plate, a glass set back in its place, a scoop of white gravy poured over a mound of potatoes, and my dad clearing his throat, no one spoke.

"Let's go upstairs, and I'll show you the children's rooms," Jean said.

We walked up the winding staircase, constructed with oversized banisters of cherry-stained wood. "I let each of our children decorate their room. Each room turned out different but nice." Her daughter's room was a pastel color, with a ruffled bedspread and stuffed animals laying about. Her son's room was blue with model airplanes and a photograph of Michael Jordan hanging on the wall. While Jean talked about her children's rooms, I just heard the sound of running feet as Keith chased my mother up the stairs. I heard the thud as something hit the floor. My body shook, and fear grabbed hold of me. I had to leave.

"Jean, I can't tell you how much this has meant to me. Would it be okay if I looked in the barn?"

"Yes, that would be fine. Take all the time you want. I'll stay here and do some work in the house."

I moved toward the stairs as quickly as I could. Jean and Paula followed.

Once Paula and I were on the front porch, the fear left me. I was ready to see the barn.

"How do you remember all of those things?" Paula asked as we walked the two hundred yards to the barn. "It was incredible. You seemed to know more about the house and the changes than Jean knew. It was like you were giving her a tour of her own house!"

Yes. It felt good. The blueprint matched, and I knew that my memories were true. When Paula and I reached the barn, I wondered what it would be like to see the site of my most vivid nightmares. As we entered, I remembered myself as a seven-year-old boy with Keith, my fourteen-year-old brother, and our cousins, John and Sammy, who lived just up the road. Keith was a good five feet eight inches tall and stood a head and a half taller than me. While we both had blond hair, that's where the similarities ended. I was shaped more like a small rectangular box weighing about sixty pounds, while Keith was leaner. I had Dad's blue eyes and thick lips. Keith's eyes were green and fixed, like my mom's. When he was mad, his thin lips turned in like two dried-up worms. John was one year shy of Keith but was about the same size. He looked up to Keith and would do anything to gain his favor. Sammy wasn't much bigger than me but was two years older and big enough to be considered one of them.

As a boy, I had mimicked the actions of my brother and two cousins at every opportunity. Regardless of what they did to me, I was their shadow, looking to gain their approval. In the summers, Dad and Uncle James took us to the fields where we cut corn stalks out of the soybeans. After Keith, John, and Sammy had sharpened their hoes to a razor's edge, they charged down each bean row while cornstalks flew every which way. With blistered hands and a hoe that stood twice my height, I continually dropped behind.

There was a time when my dad and Uncle James took us to the city to pick out baseball gloves. We rode in the back of the pickup while the men sat in the cab. Keith, John, and Sammy laughed, joked, and talked about who was the best baseball player ever, who was the toughest fighter in school, and how Sara James was growing some nice tits. I listened and learned.

After my dad parked the truck, we walked into the biggest sporting goods store I had ever seen. Dad ushered us over to the baseball gear where Keith, John, and Sammy knew just what they were looking for. Keith discussed his choice of a first baseman's glove with Dad while John and Sammy chose outfielder gloves that were big enough to snag the hardest-hit ball.

"Come on, Larry," Uncle James said. "Let's fix you up with a major league glove. You look like a catcher to me, built low to the ground. How about a Roy Campanella catcher's mitt?" I pulled the mitt down from the shelf and began ramming my fist into its pocket. "Before you go to bed tonight, I want you to rub some olive oil in the pocket of your catcher's mitt. After you've done that, push your baseball deep into the glove. Take some string and tie the glove closed until it smothers the ball. By the next morning, your glove will know how to catch any ball thrown its way."

Fifty years later, here I stood. Time had become my friend, and the memories were clearer.

I looked around the barn, squinting to make out the face of a character or to wipe away the blur from my vision. Distorted images were accompanied by fear, anxiety, and the clammy feel of cold sweat. I climbed the ladder to the hayloft. Standing there, I could recall the physical structure of the place in the minutest detail and the terrible things that had happened here. The stinging pain of my naked body being thrown across a bale of hay, hot breath on the back of my neck, screams from three jubilant boys gone wild was real. I descended from the loft and rejoined Paula, who was waiting by the foot of the ladder.

Paula turned toward me. "Are you glad we made the trip to your farm?"

"Oh yes. I'm glad you came with me. I don't know if I could have done this by myself."

Paula smiled. "Thanks for asking me. This gives me a better understanding of what you went through."

"This has to be one of the most important days of my life. Having you with me makes this experience even more meaningful. Thank you."

Together, Paula and I had strengthened our bond as we faced our joint venture: to verify the truth of my memories.

We stood inside the barn, scanning the area where so much evil was inflicted upon me as a little boy. We didn't speak as I opened the door leading to the outside. Walking into the daylight from the darkness of a dusty barn seemed to be an appropriate exit.

For months, I had studied and questioned my repressed memories that had surfaced. I needed to know whether they were true. Now that I knew they were true, I was ready to continue my recovery and the hard work that lay ahead. But as good as this emotional trip was, I'm still troubled by the fact that I didn't remember my dad ever touching me or giving me a hug. I had missed out on the physical and emotional contact I imagine happening between a father and his son. Now that I think about it, I don't remember seeing any emotional contact between my dad and his father. There seems to be a governor attached to the Franklin family that automatically limits displays of emotions.

Together, Paula and I walked back to the house. Jean sat on the front porch. "Well, how were things in the barn?" she asked.

"It certainly brought back a lot of memories."

THE BREAKUP

Seven years and five months old.

It was spring of 1950. Early evening, maybe seven o'clock, just before dinner when the chores were finished, and the sun was setting. My mother, Keith, and I were in a room just off the kitchen. While we called it the living room, a whatever-room might have been more appropriate. There was a large, wooden table covered with junk, an overstuffed chair, and two sofas covered with large, discolored sheets. A sewing machine and a kerosene stove, both considered staples in our house, occupied the rest of the room. Mom told me that in addition to food and water, the kerosene stove was the second most important thing needed to keep us alive during the cold winters in central Illinois. It was our only means of heat, but since the stove was small and couldn't heat our entire house, we kept to the first floor. Dad and Keith slept in a bedroom during the evenings while mom and I slept in a bed located on the landing next to the stairs. But in the extreme cold, we all occupied a spot close to the kerosene stove in the whatever-room.

Mom also believed that the sewing machine ranked very high in the chain of importance. Without her ability to sew, I might have been running around the farm with a bare chest during the winter. The day my mother took me to the local feed store was important for the two of us. We went to the feed store and looked at the sacks of chicken feed. Each sack was in different colors and designs and would be used to make me a new shirt. I picked the color and design that suited my taste. Now the chickens would be fed, and I would have a new shirt. We then headed home, where my mother washed the material in something that made the sack feel soft. I was always proud of those shirts, especially when I wore one to school. While Keith seemed to like the shirts, he never admitted it. He didn't act like it was a big deal.

The whatever-room was also where we gathered before dinner while waiting for Dad to come back from the fields. If he didn't come back before sunset, he would have gone to Benny's Bar and Grill at the edge of town, where Dad met Sue, the woman he would eventually love. One summer evening, while we waited in the whatever-room for Dad to come home, I was watching Keith chase our mother around the dining-room table with a hickory switch. The switch was the length of a yardstick and made a snapping sound when it hit my mother's skin. This had happened many times before. It was like watching the one-hundredth rerun of an old movie. I had no idea how long this chase would last. It depended on how quickly Keith's anger was outstripped by boredom with the whole affair or, as sometimes happened, Mom submitted and fell to the ground.

Keith was still chasing my mother when I heard Dad's footsteps climb the front porch steps. The screen door swung open and slammed shut. At the sound of the slamming door, Keith and Mom stood motionless and looked at my father as if waiting for him to pass judgment on the scene. I remember it had been hot that day, but when Dad came back from working in the fields, the whatever-room turned cold and brittle. When I think of it now, the room seemed to be a dirty, faded white, the color of four people about to die.

"What in the hell is going on?" Dad yelled. Any semblance of a breeze from the open windows died, and the switchgrass growing outside grew stiff.

My mother explained that Keith, when asked to perform his chores, beat her with a hickory switch. As my mother spoke, my dad seemed unconcerned. When she finished, he turned to walk away.

My mother called after him: "You don't love me?" That's what my mother said.

"That's right," my dad said as he turned and looked at her hard. "I don't love you." When he said this, I remember his shoulders jerked back, and he seemed to grow taller. He turned and motioned for Keith. Still gripping the hickory switch, Keith followed Dad out the door. The two of them climbed into the car and drove away. My mother sank onto the sofa and began to cry.

I remember I reached my arm around her and patted her back. If I felt anything at the time, I don't remember. As an adult, I have no memory of any feelings on my part. And yet, I patted her back to provide some comfort. Perhaps I did feel something. I will never know because all I remember now (and I remember this well) was a feeling of tapping a table while waiting for the waitress to bring the bill.

I don't remember what happened next, but Mom and I probably ate a few bites of dinner to tide us over. People don't eat a lot of food when their lives are falling apart. My mother most likely called her parents in Louisville and told them that her husband didn't love her. I do remember hearing a lot of crying and being told to go to bed. The next thing that I remember is my mother's voice the next morning: "Get dressed and take your suitcase to the front porch. Your grandfather will be here in a few minutes."

I sat up in bed to see my mother packing a suitcase and several boxes. It was barely light outside.

"What's going on?" I asked.

"Your father doesn't want us."

"What do you mean?"

"He doesn't love you. We're going to go live with your grandparents. You'd better eat something. It's going to be a while before we get another chance. There's some milk and cold cereal on the kitchen table."

It's curious the details my brain has chosen to dust off and show me after hiding them away for so long.

I remember that I pulled on my jeans and T-shirt and walked to the kitchen. I remember the milk was unusually cold, and the cereal felt like gravel in my mouth. I remember gulping water after each bite to force the food down my tightened throat. It took three or more swallows to process a single bite. I kept thinking about what my mother had said to me, *"Your father doesn't want us anymore. Your father doesn't love you."*

I finished eating the cereal and walked to the room where my mother was packing. "Take your suitcase to the front porch and wait for your grandfather to arrive," she said. Minutes later, my grandfather's 1949 Ford turned into the lane and parked in front of our house. My mother ran to the car, where they talked for a couple of minutes. Then the two of them began carrying boxes from the house to the car while I and my dog, Nippy, sat on the front porch.

My dad, followed by Keith, walked from the house to the porch. My dad looked at me, "Son, you listen to your mother and do what she says. Do you hear me?" I nodded my head while Keith looked on.

When Mom had finished packing the car, she stood on the porch with my father and Keith. The hickory switch rested against the front of the house. None of them spoke. My father never said goodbye to his wife of twenty years. Keith didn't say anything to my mother, and she never said goodbye to him, or I love you, or listen to your dad and do the right thing. Even Nippy was still. Then a slight breeze rustled the leaves of our hickory trees. Keith's hickory switch slipped from its perch and fell to the porch, and I walked with Mom and Nippy to my grandfather's car.

Seven years and eight months old.

Louisville, Illinois, some one hundred miles southeast of the farm, was the county seat for Clay County. With a population of one thousand people, a town square, and a courthouse constructed of concrete walls, marble floors, and long steps leading to a north and south entrance, Louisville seemed city-like and unfamiliar. My grandparents lived in a three-bedroom frame house on Monroe Street, one block from the elementary school and two blocks from the town square.

In the spring of 1950, my mother, Nippy, and I moved in with my grandparents in Louisville. My mother and I shared a bed in Louisville. Keith and my dad shared a bed in the two-story farmhouse.

THE WEEK MY DAD LOVED ME

1950
De Land, Illinois

It was months later, after the crops had grown from mere seeds to mature plants, when I returned to the two-story farmhouse for a one-week visit with Keith and my dad. My parents had decided that this was the right thing to do. Grandfather Tolliver and my mother took me to the farm. When we turned off Highway 16 and headed north on the De Land blacktop, we saw my father driving our way. Cars pulled to the side of the road. My father got out of his car and approached us. I cautiously stepped out of the car and walked to my father. Grandfather Tolliver opened the trunk of his car and, without looking up, quietly passed the suitcase to my father. There was no "How are you doing? Think it'll rain? Your beans look good" exchange. My mother opened her door, stood up, and faced my father. The car stood between the two of them.

"We'll be back in a week to pick him up."

"I'll have him ready."

My mother and grandfather didn't go to the farm-house to see Keith even though it was no more than a mile down the road. Maybe my mother didn't want to see him. Perhaps she was afraid of him. Even to this day, I wonder why a mother would choose not to see her son.

As I drove to the farm with my father, I wondered what was next. Dad and I had never spent much time together. He was either working in the fields or at Benny's Bar and Grill. We turned right onto the lane leading to the house, which sported a chilling look for a 90-degree day. The front screen door swung open and slammed shut as Keith swaggered across the porch, stood at the edge, looked to the left, to the right, and focused his eyes on me.

While my dad walked up the steps, I latched onto his right hip, keeping my dad between Keith and me. Keith never said a word, but his eyes made contact with mine. After dropping off the suitcase, my father said, "You boys get in the car. I've got to run some errands." Since the separation, Dad had begun racing his 1948 Ford in local stock car races. Racing cars had been Dad's dream, but Mom had complained of the cost and thought it was silly. Now, Dad and Keith spent endless evening hours in the machine shed working on their car.

On the way to the machine shop, Keith sat in the passenger seat, and I sat between him and Dad. We sped down the dry, gravel road, which yearned for summer rain. From a distance, the car must have looked like a small dot racing across the countryside.

"Why don't you move over onto my lap and drive for a while," my dad said.

I couldn't believe my ears, but I quickly slid over and grabbed the steering wheel while Dad pushed down on the accelerator. The back tires spun, and gravel flew out the back. Keith pressed his face against the windshield; he didn't know the meaning of fear. The car fishtailed on the gravel road as I struggled to keep control of the car. Sometimes the wheels kicked up so much dust it covered the windshield like a chalky fog. Dad let me drive all the way to our destination. As the three of us climbed from the car, Dad and Keith laughed and agreed that I had done a good job.

My memory of the first night sleeping at the house is of a single moment. While Keith and Dad were already in bed, I stood at the end of the bed watching the two of them. I didn't know what to do. My dad looked at me and laughed. "Larry, don't just stand there. Hop in bed with us." I undressed down to my underwear and crawled in between the two of them. Dad thought it was funny, but Keith was not pleased. Perhaps he felt uncomfortable with me sleeping next to Dad. Maybe he thought that Dad was giving me too much attention. Since Keith and I never talked, the reasons for his behavior were unclear. I always avoided him. Staring at him invited his wrath, and I was careful never to wake him.

Dad made certain that Keith and I were never left together during my one-week visit, and Keith never talked to me after that first day when Dad let me drive the car. I heard him talk to our cousins, but I'm certain he never talked to me. I later learned that there were times when Dad spent a lot of time with his girlfriend. My uncle, who lived up the road, said that he would hear Keith shooting a shotgun throughout the night. Sometimes, when Dad returned to the farm in the early morning hours, Keith was still outside, shooting the shotgun at anything that moved. Those nights must have been lonely for a fourteen-year-old boy.

A few days later, on Friday night, the three of us drove to the racetrack in Dad's old pickup truck that pulled the stock car. While Dad walked me to the grandstand where his brothers and their families were sitting, I listened as he and Keith rattled off a list of modifications they had made to the engine and suspension system, increasing the car's acceleration and ability to hang into a curve. It had rained during the day, and I overheard them talking about how the mud would be flying. We got to the grandstands, and he left me with my three uncles and their families to cheer for him while he raced. Keith walked back to the track with Dad and remained in the pit stop during the race.

Some thirty minutes later, the cars took their warm-up laps and moved into their predetermined positions. Next came the downward movement of a flag, and the race was on. The engines roared as the cars labored through each turn, digging out chunks of mud that were hurled into the stands. Despite the morning shower, the officials had spread water on the track so some mud would make it into the stands. It became obvious to me why Dad enjoyed racing. It demanded a certain aggression and lack of fear, both traits of my father. He led most of the race and would have won if his car hadn't overheated going into the final lap. He eased up on the accelerator and settled for third place. While the winning purse for third place was small, it was enough to fuel his desire to continue stock car racing until he died eight weeks later.

During my visit, every day was one of a series of scorchers without a trace of a cloud to soften the heat. Cornstalks struggled to stand, and soybeans were wrinkled, like the face of an old man. While the racetrack had heavy rain the night before, Dad's farm, some twenty miles south, still needed a slow summer rain. I was pleased but surprised when Dad said, "Hey, Larry, how about you and me go to town for a cold bottle of soda pop?" I never remembered being asked that before. Keith was always the one Dad took to town. But this time, Keith stayed home.

Dad and I climbed into the pickup and headed south toward Benny's Bar and Grill. I hung my arm out the window as the wind blew hard against my skin, causing the tiny hairs to stand upward. When we arrived, he took me to the long bar with stools that swiveled each time I moved my butt from side to side. Dad rested his feet on a long silver pipe at the base of the bar. My feet hung in the air like Monday's wash. Behind us were a few booths with bright red plastic seats and silver-gray tabletops spotted with cigarette burns. My dad ordered a tall, dark bottle of beer and a half-frozen bottle of Coke for me. He also ordered two cake donuts covered with white powdered sugar that stuck to my lips each time I took a bite. Men stopped by the long countertop to talk with my dad about the need for a summer rain, his stock car racing, and if I was his boy.

Sue, a waitress at the bar and grill, dried off her wet hands with a dish towel and walked our way. She was twelve years younger than my dad and, unlike my mother, brought excitement to a conversation even if it was meant just to pass the time of day. Sue believed that there was more to life than cooking, sewing, and doing the chores. It was no secret that my dad loved her.

"This is Larry, my younger boy," Dad said as he looked my way. Sue commented on how cute I was and how I looked like my dad. All I could manage was a "hi" and my biggest smile while swinging side to side on the metal stool. Sue had an ease in the way she moved, her soft eyes, and her shapely figure. My dad and Sue talked in near whispers like couples do. I turned in my stool, listened to the farmers laugh, watched them drink coffee, and then sit back, taking deep pulls from their cigarettes. I wanted to be a farmer like my dad. He worked on some days and drank beer and coffee on other days. I decided I would do the same.

Keith was the one who always went with Dad to the fields, but there was one time when I rode the tractor with Dad as he disked a freshly plowed field. I sat in his lap while he wrapped his left arm around my waist and held me tight. He even allowed me to hold onto the steering wheel. A couple of times, I turned the wrong way, but my dad didn't get mad. We just turned around and redid the spots I had missed. Dad seemed like a different person then, and now that my parents were about to be divorced and my dad was going to marry Sue, he seemed more like that person again. I was beginning to love this man my dad had become.

We finished the week by going to Sue's home for Sunday's dinner. The intent was to spend some time with Sue and Janet, her eight-year-old daughter. As we entered Sue's home, the table was set for Dad, Sue, Janet, Keith, and me. If not for the car accident that killed them all but Janet, I imagine this would have been my new family. There was a large table covered with a nice tablecloth and freshly polished silverware. I had never seen so much food. Janet was quiet, but she seemed okay, and Sue was especially nice.

It should have been a nice evening, but Keith did not put any food on his plate, not even a single bite. I sat at the table and didn't move. I couldn't move. I was unable to pick up a fork, lift a glass or say a single word. I followed Keith's lead in everything he did and didn't eat a single bite of food. Sue looked confused, and my dad didn't say anything to either of us. The look on his face was sadder than anything I had ever seen.

My behavior at Sue's house was terrible. And Sue was the woman my dad loved. But I had no choice. I followed Keith's lead, the brother who beat me and raped me.

September 4, 1950

Louisville, Illinois

It was September 4th, six weeks after my visit with my dad. I was in the second grade. I had walked the one block from school and moved up the steps to my grandparent's home. My mother and grandmother were sitting at the kitchen table, gripping their coffee cups hard. They began speaking with whispered words. My mother rose from the table and led me into the bedroom, where she told me to sit down. She had something to say.

"Keith and your dad were in a car wreck. They were traveling to the state fair. Your dad was driving fast and ran into a truck pulling a horse trailer. Your dad and Keith were both killed, but they didn't feel a thing. And your grandfather Franklin, your cousin Rita Joyce and your dad's girlfriend were killed too. We're going to De Land tomorrow to stay with your Uncle James and Aunt Wanda. The funeral will be the next day. You sit in here, pull yourself together, and come to the kitchen. We'll be eating soon."

No one talked around the dinner table that night. Chewing our food and forcing ourselves to swallow was all that could be expected. The quiet was interrupted by my mother: "Mrs. Valley will drive us to De Land tomorrow. You had better go to bed early and get some rest. You're going to need it." Mrs. Valley, a second-grade teacher, had lost her husband two years before and was now my mother's best friend.

My recollections of that night are spotty, but I remember turning on the radio that sat on the night-stand next to the bed I shared with my mother. While the electronic voices usually put me to sleep, this night was different. I spent the night resting my head on a wet pillow.

The next morning my mom and I dressed in the dark and only spoke when necessary. As the sun slowly appeared over the trees, Mrs. Valley drove her car onto my grandparent's gravel driveway. My mother had packed our suitcases while I slept, and she had them ready to load into the trunk. After she arranged them, she gave me a pillow so I could sleep in the backseat. I pretended to sleep while my mother and Mrs. Valley talked about how hot a summer we'd had, how cold of a winter we were supposed to have, and how my mother made some changes in a pattern she found at Martha's Fabric store.

Two hours later, we turned off Highway 16 outside of De Land and headed up the blacktop road leading to Uncle James's house. On the way, we passed Dad's farmhouse. I leaned forward in the backseat, hoping to see my father walk across the lawn in his khaki pants and a white T-shirt or maybe see Keith standing on the front porch. My mother turned to look at the farmhouse as well, but the house stood still.

We soon turned onto the road to Uncle James's house. So many cars were parked on the lane that some had pulled onto the front yard. I remember their house, particularly the sound of the tin roof when it rained. Two dogs greeted us with their barks and wiggles, followed by uncles, aunts, and cousins. While my mother and Mrs. Valley followed the women into the house, I stayed outside with the men sharing photos of my father's flattened car. It was squashed like one of those boxy shuttle cars used to transport coal miners in and out of underground mines. No one could have survived that, someone said. Someone else told the late arrivals how the accident occurred. "Wendall was traveling south on Highway 54. He was behind a truck that was pulling a horse trailer and going real slow. Wendall went to pass it, and just then, the truck turned left in front of Wendall's car. He couldn't stop. His car drove right under the truck, killed two horses, and cut off the top of his car. The hood was pushed backward, cutting off his head and hitting Keith right in the forehead, smashing it back a good three inches. The front seat was pushed back and broke Keith's legs off. His heels were right up under the back of his knees; bones were sticking out every which way." Someone else said that my dad was so strong it took a crowbar to pry his hands from the steering wheel. This celebration of my dad's strength and bravery was as strange and unexpected to me as the remarks about his gruesome death. No one mentioned that my dad had been speeding, as reported in the newspaper.

I'd slipped into a stupor, as I recall, when Uncle Henry pulled me to the side. "Your father owes me some money, and I want to settle up. I took his shotgun that is worth about a hundred dollars. I've got two of his watches. One is as good as new, but the other watch was on your father at the time of the wreck and has a smashed crystal. It shows you the exact time your father was killed. Which one do you want? I'll keep the other, and we can call it even." He waited as I looked over the watches and rubbed my fingers over the broken crystal.

"I'll keep this one with a smashed face."

Uncle Henry nodded and pocketed the working watch. Then he patted my head and walked away. I still have the watch, its hands stopped at 9:17 am.

I spent the rest of the day walking around direction-less, listening to the adults talk. Occasionally, one of the uncles gave me a pat on my head, or an aunt walked by, looked down at me, and when her eyes leaked tears, she hurried away.

Mother, Mrs. Valley, and I spent the night at Uncle James' house. The following day, a steady stream of people loaded into their cars and caravanned to the funeral home. My mother, Mrs. Valley, and I sat in Uncle James' car, which was so quiet that I could count the RPMs as the car accelerated from first to second and then second to third. Even Uncle James, who was considered a good driver, nervously ground the gears. James and my father were close.

We arrived at the funeral home, a large two-story brick house with massive concrete steps leading to the main entrance. Organ music and the smell of flowers slipped out each time the door opened. Inside the reception room, four caskets sat high off the floor, and each held a stone-gray object. Each casket was draped with individual banners naming the occupant: grandfather, cousin, brother, father. Not being an official member of the Franklin family, Sue was to have a separate funeral the next day.

We moved from one body to another. Their skin was covered with white powder; their lips were bleached, and their hair was coarse, like horsehair. The women, with tissues in hand, examined the flowers and speculated on the cost. They consoled each other with meaningless phrases. *He looks so nice. It's a blessing. God called them home. They're better off.* Grandfather Franklin's body was the least upsetting. He was old, and death was expected. But my cousin, Rita Joyce, was only twelve years old and should not have died. Now she was limp and empty.

My mother walked up to Keith and, for the first time, stared him down. It was hard to tell if she cried since she used one tissue the entire day. For me, Keith did not look as lifeless and gray as the others. He looked like a jack-in-the-box, ready to jump out at any time. I was afraid to move closer to him. I could not be certain that he was dead.

The two cousins who hung out with Keith and me sat in chairs in front of the caskets. Both cried with louder moans than I would have expected, but since I didn't know how to cry, I took their lead and moaned loudly too. My mother told me to stop as if I was doing something wrong, so I stopped.

My aunt began whispering like she had important information she was eager to share with my mother. The whispered words were loud enough for me to hear: my aunt had been wondering where Sue's body was stored. My aunt had noticed a locked door that had a keyhole large enough to look through. She saw Sue's naked body sitting in a reclining chair, waiting to be prepared for tomorrow's funeral, and was anxious to tell my mother what she saw. She didn't hesitate to tell how scary Sue looked. In hindsight, I can only imagine that there might have been a shade of satisfaction since Sue was the one who stole my father.

Of the four caskets, the uncles were all gathered around the biggest. One of them looked up, tipped his head toward the casket, and said, "Hey, Larry, here's your dad." I walked over to join him.

Laid out in a suit and tie, hair slicked down with Wildroot Cream Oil, was a man with chalk-colored skin, dead lips, and what looked like a fishnet draped over his face. The man's hair was not wavy like my father's. This man looked scary. Perhaps this was not my father. Then Grandmother Franklin, who had insisted on an open casket even though my father had been decapitated, walked up to the casket, pulled back the fishnet from this dead man's face, held its hands, and then kissed its face. Everyone watched in silence. I looked again at that man in the box who was not my father and wondered if maybe my father had died when he put me in bed with my mother.

After the viewing, we gathered outside the funeral home and formed a caravan behind three hearses. It was a two-hour trip down winding roads to the country cemetery five miles southeast of Louisville, close to where my father was raised.

The cemetery was at the top of a small hill. On the way, we passed a pond that had run dry. Remnants of dead fish were stuck in the mud. In the middle of the cemetery was a large, half-dead sycamore tree. I wondered if some lost souls buried six feet below had sucked the life out of that pond. And why didn't my mother's parents come to the cemetery to pay their respects? The cemetery was only a thirty-minute drive from their house. Decades passed, and they never mentioned Dad's name, but grandmother did say to me: "You don't know how lucky you are that your Dad and Keith were killed." I wonder now how much she knew.

Everybody got out of their cars and walked quietly to a spot where four freshly dug holes waited. The men carried each casket across the ground, lowering one at a time into their grave. With all four in place, a preacher, dressed in his Sunday suit and carrying his overused Bible, said some mumble-jumble about them going to meet the Lord. As I watched my father and brother lying side by side, I overheard my mother whisper to Mrs. Valley that there were no more burial plots left. My anxiety increased as I wondered what would happen to me when I died. Where would they put me? Maybe when I die, they could put me on top of my dad. The hole seemed deep enough. At that moment, I realized that once again, I had been left out. Keith got his way and would sleep with my Dad forever. My lungs locked up tight, my heartbeat slowed, and I could barely breathe. I willed myself to die, but the nature of life forced my body to move, my mind to think, and, involuntarily, I lived.

Soon after the death of my father and brother, I often rose from my bed and wandered throughout the house, dressed in my jockey shorts, and sporting a glassy-eyed stare. I don't know what was going through my mind on those nights. On each occasion, someone led me back to bed, where I remained for the rest of the night. My mother and grandparents considered sleepwalking humorous and, like a pair of old shoes, something that I would outgrow.

It was a Saturday night in late November when a gospel concert was being held at the Louisville Grade

School Gymnasium. By placing folding chairs on the floor, the gymnasium expanded its seating capacity to over three hundred people. My mother and grandmother, lifetime fans of gospel music, had planned to attend the concert that would begin at 8:00 pm and go well into the night. My grandfather agreed to stay home with me and was instructed to lock all the doors so I wouldn't leave the house if I began to sleepwalk.

At 10:30 pm, I pulled back my blanket, crawled out of bed, and began my familiar stroll throughout the house. But this night was different. I walked to the back door and saw the key left in the lock. I opened the door, walked down the steps, turned left, and moved across the gravel driveway to Madison Street, which led to the gymnasium some two blocks away.

That night was a cold, winter night with a forecast of a heavy frost—too cold for snow, the weatherman had said. My path that night was probably followed by the huffs-and-puffs of air from my mouth each time I exhaled, but I didn't feel the cold, nor the sting of small rocks on the bottom of my bare feet, nor did I remember the darkness being interrupted by the streetlights hanging at each intersection. But I do remember that the gymnasium was filled with people talking and listening to the Gospel Land Quartet singing "Mansion on the Hilltop."

I pushed the door open as a wave of people turned to look in my direction. A stranger wrapped his trench coat around my nearly naked body. Minutes later, my

mother and grandmother walked across the gymnasium floor for all to see while the Gospel Quartet began
singing "Amazing Grace."

With a stern voice and a troubled face, my mother
thanked the stranger for the use of his coat while wrap-
ping her coat around me. The walk back to our house
was silent as my mother and grandmother most likely
wondered how this could happen and how embarrassing this was.

As I crawled back into bed, my mother looked down
at me. "What's wrong with you?"

"I don't know," I said.

TROUBLED BEHAVIOR

1955–1958
Louisville, Illinois

My mother and I lived with her parents for over a year. It was during this time that I bonded with my grandfather Tolliver, who I called Pop. I had a close relationship with him, but there was a certain distance between my grandmother and myself. I believe it had something to do with her emphasis on discipline and housework. Each night she listed the tasks for the following day and made assignments for who would do what. She had no patience for anyone who didn't complete their work on the assigned day.

There was an uncomfortable time when my grandmother, mother, and I were outside while I was washing the car. On this particular day, Pop was plowing a field and wouldn't be home until the end of the day. Time was not a luxury for farmers who were dependent upon the weather. You work when the weather permits. My grandmother had been complaining to Pop that some oil on the side of the car needed to be removed. The car was a 1955 Chevy that was a beauty. My grandmother should have given Pop some extra time to get the crops in. But she didn't have the patience to wait for anything. Not knowing how to remove oil from the car, she thought it best to use SOS pads. She dipped a couple of SOS pads in a bucket of water. The suds bubbled up while she rubbed hard and long. Feeling good about herself, she turned the water on and began washing off the suds to see the finished project. As soon as the soap was removed, the oil and paint were gone as well. My grandmother saw her mistake.

That night when Pop returned home for some food and a little time to rest, he checked out his car that appeared to have been washed. It was the first time I had ever seen Pop this upset. He couldn't speak. Instead, he drove the car to the dealer the next morning and traded for another 1955 Chevy. Of course, he had to face ridicule from everyone at the dealer who witnessed the job his wife had done to his car.

A large garden reminded my grandparents that you would always have something to eat if you cared for your garden. To do otherwise was a sin. On this day, my grandmother pointed out some work in the garden that needed doing. When I agreed to do the work tomorrow and didn't want to do it today, she snapped. She slapped me across the face, rattling my jaw. As I walked towards her with a closed fist, my mother quickly stepped between the two of us. A few days later, my mother told me that she would be looking for a house of our own. She thought it was too much for all of us to be living in the same house. A month later, she followed up on her promise.

I think my mother and grandmother viewed my father and me as the same: "two peas in a pod," they called me. They knew I was an angry boy in my early years and drank a lot in my teenage years. The fact that Dad and I looked alike was a constant reminder that I was his son. Even though my father had abandoned me, I missed him. I wanted to get to know him better; to have him call me by my given name, Larry; to teach me how to drive the tractor and plant corn in a freshly manicured field and tell me that he loved me more than a little. But I sometimes wondered what would have happened to me if my parents were still together and Keith was still alive.

It was after my Grandmother Tolliver's death that I understood her stern ways. It was just after she was put to rest, and I was outside her house talking with my mother's brother, Warren Tolliver, and Paul, a distant relative.

"It was a real shame what happened to your Grandmother Pansy when she was a child," Paul said.

"What are you talking about?" I asked.

"Oh, you don't know what happened with her dad?"

Warren and I looked at each other. We shook our heads.

Paul went on. "Well, Pansy's dad, Alvey, was an alcoholic and got real mean when he was drunk. Alvey had spent the entire day at a local bar, and Pansy's mother,

Emma, took Pansy and her brother Carl to a neighbor's house for safety.

"The next day, they went back to the house. Alvey wasn't there, but there was a mess of blood in the kitchen, so Emma took the kids right back to the neighbor's house. When the neighbors went to investigate, they found an old .22 caliber pistol in the kitchen and a blood trail leading out the back. They followed it and found Alvey's body hanging from the hayloft in the barn."

I gasped. My ace-in-the-hole. "Suicide?"

Paul nodded. "They cut down the body and there was a bullet wound in Alvey's head. Alvey must have come home, seen his wife and kids gone, and used the pistol on himself. The bullet went into his head but didn't kill him. So he went to the barn where he hanged himself."

I was stunned. I'd imagined killing myself for years, but I had not imagined it could be so hard to do it right. I pressed Paul. "How did he survive a gunshot wound to the head?" I asked.

"A .22 has a small caliber, Larry. Not a lot of power there."

"But he would have known that," I argued. "And a .22 tends to have more than one round." I shook my head. "I don't know. If I were gonna kill myself with a .22, I'd load more than a single round."

Paul shrugged. "I guess, but we're talking about suicide. That's not exactly rational."

I dropped the subject.

When I saw my mother later, I told her what I'd heard. "Is that true?" I asked. "Did Grandmother Tolliver's dad really shoot himself and then hang himself in the barn?"

"Yes."

"Why didn't you ever tell me this? Is there anything else I should know?"

"I thought everybody knew about it. No, there's nothing else to tell," she said. I wanted to know more, but my mother dismissed me as if this were no big thing, just as she would do a decade later when I asked her to share information about my physical and sexual abuse.

Baptized in the
Wabash River

1955
Louisville, Illinois

In Louisville, Illinois, life and death were viewed through the prism of the Southern Baptist Church—a small, brick building with white trim and a modest steeple—located one block from the town square. A handful of mom-and-pop stores, a barbershop, and a pool hall where boys become men circled the square. The church was my self-imposed sanctuary on Sunday mornings. Sunday school from 9:30 to 10:30 am, church service from 11:00 am to 12:00 pm, prayer meetings on Wednesday evenings, Bible school in the summer, and a weeklong revival two times a year exceeded my appetite for the Lord.

I've always remembered the evening service when I was "saved." The choir and congregation sang the seductive sounds of "Amazing Grace." The minister stood at the front of the church while inviting lost souls to confess their sins. I don't understand how it happened. I was singing my favorite church hymn, and then I felt an unbelievable force "calling me home." It challenged me to slide out of the pew and reach out to the minister, while another competing force challenged me to stay where I was. I chose to be saved.

My mother was at the church that night, and she seemed to enjoy the attention she gained from my confession and that I had been saved. For some reason, my grandparents were not there. I couldn't wait until the next morning when I could tell my grandmother that I had been "saved." I knew she would be proud of me.

The next morning I ran down the basement stairs to where my grandmother was washing the laundry.

"Grandma, did you hear what happened to me last night?"

"No, what are you talking about?"

"I was saved."

She turned and continued washing the laundry. To my surprise, there were no congratulations, a hug, or I'm glad you were saved, or someday you're going to Heaven. She simply looked at the laundry and continued to sort the colored clothes from the whites.

A few weeks later, I was taken to the Wabash River, where I was baptized. The minister lowered me into the river, much like a man dunking his donut into a cup of coffee. It seemed strange that I had to be submerged in the Wabash River, a place I feared, or I wouldn't be saved. I'm not sure what this experience did for me. But I did what was expected, and I didn't drown.

I always had a bit of anxiety when I swam in the river with my friends. Not knowing what might be below the surface was troublesome. The fear that someone or something might pull me under and do bad things to me was always there. Sometimes my friends and I went to the Wabash River, where we had a rope attached to a large limb that hung over the river. We took turns swinging over the river and letting go of the rope. When I fell into the river, I swam to the bank as fast as possible and jumped as quickly as I could out of the water. The fear didn't extend to my time spent in the local pool where the water was clear, enabling me to see what was below the surface. While time spent in the swimming pool was fun, the river scared me.

Now that I was saved, the church offered redemption from my sins and guidance on issues of life and death. For me, the life part held little interest, but death drew me in. Although I viewed death as cold and violent, I appreciated the finality that it offered. Death was like the end of a sentence with a brief separation before the next sentence begins. If life became unbearable, death was a welcomed possibility.

Five years after my father, brother, cousin, and grandfather died, Mr. Lively, my grade-school band teacher, was also killed in a car accident. He had all the qualities of kindness and understanding I wanted in a father. He heaped praise on my musical abilities when I completed three lessons after he'd assigned only one. Mr. Lively was my imaginary dad for three years before he moved on to a bigger school and better pay. He never told me why he was leaving. He just disappeared.

I never talked to or about him until a year later when my mother walked into my bedroom to break the news.

"Mr. Lively is dead. They said he had been drinking and drove his car into a telephone pole. He was killed immediately, probably didn't feel a thing. I heard he and his wife were having problems. He was drinking a lot and probably drove his car into the telephone pole on purpose."

My reaction was a mere one-syllable word. "Oh."

"Do you want to go to his funeral?"

"No."

Looking back, I must have experienced feelings of abandonment when Mr. Lively left me. Another father chose to leave me.

L.D. Legg was a high school friend who saw death earlier than most. Although we had never discussed it, we must have recognized deep-seated emotional problems in each other, for we often self-medicated with beer on secluded country roads. One Saturday, after L.D. had spent the evening drinking beer in the parking lot of a local restaurant, he got tired of waiting for me and left. When I arrived at the restaurant parking lot that night, I was told that L.D. had been looking for me. I waited for an hour or so, thinking that he would appear, but he never did. I drove home sober.

On Sunday morning, my mother made another trip to my bedroom to inform me that L.D. was dead. He had wrecked his car while driving in a drunken stupor down one of those dark, country roads. I managed to ask how it happened and then rolled over and went back to sleep. It wasn't until hours later when I woke and met with some of my friends to sort through the details. L.D.'s car had been towed to the local body shop. The front and back were smashed, leaving massive bloodstains on the front seat. I touched his blood which was a darker color than I had imagined. We circled the mangled car and speculated that his death was quick and that he probably didn't feel a thing. Well, that's what everyone said as we stared at the cloud-like patches of blood and minute pieces of human flesh.

I couldn't attend the wake of my best friend. Supporting his parents as they dealt with the grief and sadness was unthinkable. But since I was asked to be a pallbearer, I had no choice but to attend his funeral. My mind floated throughout the service with no more attention to what was happening around me than if I were standing in the checkout line at the grocery store. I do remember that the minister looked at me throughout his sermon. He probably knew that L.D. had been drinking beer while waiting for me. Perhaps he knew that I'd had a date that night, and if I had passed on the final kiss, L.D. would be alive today.

Though I pondered the implications of my choices on the cause of L.D.'s death, I never felt the depth of sadness I knew was expected when you lose a friend. Not with L.D. or Mr. Lively. I noticed how others handled the passing of a loved one, and their grief was greater than mine.

Even in my adult years, when I was in my thirties, I attempted to measure my level of grief. If someone I loved died, would I cry? How much sadness would I feel? Would it weigh me down? I wanted to know, so one night, I imagined that my two daughters had died. I imagined everyone I knew crying for them. I imagined never seeing them again, and then I fell asleep. Sometime in the middle of the night, I woke up to discover that my pillow was damp. Not wet, just damp. It didn't represent the level of grief that I would have expected.

The Forbidden Memory

March 1999
Louisville, Illinois

For most of my life, I had no memories of my childhood, and I didn't question it. Why would I? I didn't
know any better. My past was as sterile and artificial
as a sheet of polyethylene—a vast expanse of nothing.
When my mother told me in October 1992 that my
father didn't love me, she essentially dumped a 3,000-
piece jigsaw puzzle into that empty past and left me
to put it together. With Olivia's help, I began sifting
through the pieces. I wanted confirmation that the
picture I was putting together was accurate. My dad
and brother were gone—I couldn't ask them—and I
hadn't spoken to my cousins or their family since the
funeral. So I kept pestering my mother. I pleaded with
her. I told her I thought I was going crazy, and could
she please just tell me if anything I was remembering
was true. She was sympathetic, but she wouldn't help.
Or maybe she couldn't.

She told me that soon after her divorce, she began
talking with the local chiropractor about thoughts of

committing suicide. The chiropractor had a reputation in the community for helping people who struggled with negative thoughts, and his followers were true believers in his ability to make all your pain go away. Not just physical, but emotional pain. My mother told me that he spent a year telling her to forget all the bad things that happened in her life, and they would disappear as if they never happened. To be successful, he said, she had to keep them locked away and never think of them again. "You see," she said, "I put all that behind me. It was just hurting me, and now I don't even remember what it was. It's not important." She insisted she remembered nothing and that it wouldn't help to discuss it even if she did.

"If you can't share more information," I said, "I'll have to contact my cousins. They'll have some answers." My mother didn't know that I was bluffing about contacting my cousins. I wasn't talking to them at the time and was not in an emotional state where I could confront them. But what I said shocked her. She quickly answered my threat.

"No, don't do that. It's not safe to talk with them."

"What do you mean it's not safe?"

"They might hurt you."

"What makes you say that?"

"There was a time when your cousin John threatened to shoot his sister-in-law. I was told that John was having an affair with someone. John told his sister-in-law that he would shoot her with a shotgun if she ever told his wife about the affair."

While I had no way of knowing if her story was true, my mother had no doubts, so I pressed her. "Well, tell me something, so I don't have to talk with him." Her response was a nonsequitur that confirmed the validity of my memories—a denial that pointed at the truth.

"I didn't know what was going on in the barn! All of you boys spent a lot of time in the hayloft. But I do know that you had those red marks all over your body from the hay. I had you undress so your dad could see the marks on your skin. But your dad didn't care."

In her insistence that she didn't know what was going on in the barn, it was clear that she knew something had happened there. My mother had suspected, and that is why she didn't want to leave me with Keith and my cousins when she and my dad went to Farmer City for a Saturday night dance. She may not have known exactly what my brother and cousins were doing to me, but she knew they were doing something.

Memories, dreams, and the occasional nugget of information from my mother, often shared unintentionally, all provided clues to my past. At the same time, long-term therapy showed me the way forward. In the beginning, these previously repressed memories fell into one of three categories:

(1) The Certain. Oh yes, I remember the night when my parents agreed their love had run its course.

(2) The Curious. My mother woke me the next morning and told me that Dad didn't want me? Can that be true?

(3) The Shocking but Believable. My brother and cousin repeatedly raped me and otherwise sexually abused me. Horrifying, but the memories are too vivid, too visceral to be false.

Then, in early 1999, six and a half years into therapy, I discovered a fourth category of memory: The Unbelievable. There is only one memory in this category, and it's one that forced me to consider that maybe I wasn't the kind of man I imagined myself to be.

It begins with a pickup parked in the driveway when I was thirteen years old.

———

Thirteen years old.

I had finished my Saturday evening shift at the local grocery store. It was early fall. The sky was blooming with stars. After the three-block walk to my home, I saw a pickup truck sitting in our driveway. *That must be Bill Barn's truck,* I thought.

Mr. Barn had taken my mother on a couple of dates. She mentioned that he had a new pickup. Not wanting to meet him, I sat on the back porch next to a large maple tree, watching the moon filter through the bare branches. To the south of our property line sat a telephone pole with a vapor light that allowed me to survey the neighborhood as I waited for Mr. Barn to leave. I couldn't help but wonder why my mother had gone out with a man. After all, I was doing everything a man should do. Why did she need someone else? Over the past six years, this was the third time my mother had gone out with another man. Why would she want to start dating now?

It was 10:30 pm. I knew that because our neighbor, Mrs. Lewis, always turned out her lights when the evening news was over. I felt a chill and studied each exhale that left my mouth. The only sounds were the occasional bursts of laughter that escaped from inside the house. Thirty minutes later, the front door opened, and the steps of a good-sized man sounded across the porch. He pulled open his truck door, started the engine, backed out of the driveway, and drove away. I waited a few minutes before entering the house. I didn't want my mother to know that I had been sitting on the back porch.

The next morning, I woke up early and walked to the local barbershop to get a haircut. It was the mid-1950s when barbershops were for men only, and I enjoyed hearing the latest Louisville gossip. By the time I returned home, I assumed my mother would be up, and I was looking forward to breakfast. But when I opened the front door, the house was quiet and seemed empty. I noticed that the bathroom door was closed. I knocked on the door. After no response, I pushed the door open. Naked with beads of water clinging to her body was my mother. She stood with a slight smile across her face. Seconds later, she closed the door, only to open it again. We were ghost-like figures playing a predetermined role. No words were spoken.

She was covered in a white, terry-cloth robe as I followed her into the bedroom.

She opened her robe.

———

This memory of my mother walking into her bedroom came to me often and in short bursts, like flashbacks. But each time I walked into her bedroom, just a shell of a boy following her cue, everything went black, and I couldn't help wondering what, if anything, happened.

The first time I asked Olivia to help me explore this recurring dream, she seemed reluctant. Finally, she agreed to focus on the part of the dream when I entered my mother's bedroom. As I had done many times before, I closed my eyes and envisioned the setting we were about to examine. I then waited for a scene to be developed in my mind. I focused on my mother's bedroom: the furniture, the walls, and even the bed. Sometimes the scene formed quickly. Other times I had limited success. Throughout the process, Olivia asked me to share what I was feeling and seeing. By watching my physical reactions—facial expression and the tension or lack thereof in my body—Olivia was more able to capture my emotions.

The bedroom was black, not allowing me to see what happened next. After repeated efforts, the room lightened. As I leaned forward to get a clearer view, my stomach muscles tightened, and my body shook.

"Relax," Olivia said. "Let it go. Nothing will hurt you. Tell me what you see."

I responded flatly: "I saw myself as a young teenage boy having sex with my mother." After several seconds passed, I spoke again. "Do you think that I really had sex with my mother?" I felt overcome by the sadness and questioned my value as a human being.

While Olivia didn't answer my question, she was quick to reassure me. "Don't make any judgments on the validity of what you saw. These are the feelings stored in your mind, and that's what we have to deal with. Our prime objective is to deal with the emotions. Those are more important than determining whether every detail of a memory is true."

"Just the suggestion of considering the validity of some recollections makes me so sick that I sometimes want to spit up a mouthful of vomit. The memory of Keith and Dad sharing the same bed is one of those."

"What do you mean?"

"It was when I slept with my mother, and Keith slept with my dad."

There was a look of concern on Olivia's face. "Take a few breaths and tell me what happened."

"Dad and Keith were sleeping in their bed while my mother and I were in the second bed. For some reason, I was curious to see what was going on in my dad's bedroom." I took a couple of breaths and exhaled slowly. "I made my way from my bed across the living room to the wooden pair of doors that opened much like a sliding barn door. Not wanting to wake them, I looked through a crack between the two doors. Keith was lying on his stomach, and my dad was on top. Keith saw me peeking through the crack, of that I'm certain. Our eyes met as I scurried to leave before Dad saw me. I returned to my bed without ever telling what I had seen. Even today, the only thing that resides in my mind is the look on Keith's face—an intense and angry, red face."

"I'm sorry that you have so much sadness. It's difficult to deal with decades-old memories. In time you will become more desensitized to the emotions that surface. Let's spend some quiet time and allow yourself to relax and feel at peace."

The session ended, and I felt emotionally drained. Olivia had warned me that since they had stirred up powerful emotions, I might experience some sleep disturbance. As it turned out, my exhaustion moved me into a deep sleep where I lay undisturbed until the alarm clock rattled its way across my nightstand.

But the next evening was different. Early into the night, I dreamed that a poisonous spider had bitten me. I was paralyzed. As I lay motionless, I saw myself lying in bed after having just returned from my mother's bedroom. The image—a young teenage boy smothered with guilt—continued. I begged for death but was denied. I watched the tormented boy until the morning sunlight overcame the darkness.

After exploring this dream with Olivia, I went to visit my mother. There were questions to be asked. I was desperate and needed some answers. After some small talk, I began.

"I'm still seeing my psychologist. I've had dreams of the two of us having sex together." My voice cracked. "Sometimes, I think I'm going crazy. I need some answers. Did we ever have sex together?"

"No, you're not going crazy," she assured me. My mother looked down toward the floor, paused for a few seconds as she searched for an answer. Then, as if I'd asked her if it had snowed last Christmas, she said, "Well, I don't know. I don't remember that."

I had expected her to scream and yell that nothing like that had ever happened. That she was shocked that I would ask such a thing. I had expected a denial, but instead, I got ambivalence. What else could this mean but the unthinkable?

A Sacred Journey

Early 2000s
Makanda, Illinois

I was a gnat in the forest, barely visible to the naked eye. No one knew me, and I scarcely recognized myself. Until just a few years ago, life as I knew it had begun at my father and brother's funeral when I was seven. Now, I was deluged by a flood of memories that gave me nightmares accompanied by dry heaves. I began to accept that my past included being beaten and raped multiple times as a child and that my father had chosen to love my brother instead of me. But the possibility that I'd had sex with my mother was so unimaginable that thinking about it now makes me want to vomit. Still, it was too bizarre and too specific not to be believed. In the beginning, Olivia was the sole audience to my hidden stories, most too awful to share.

I struggled with what memories to believe. How could I trust a mind that had lied to me for so long? Would I ever know the truth? And even those memories I believed, who could I tell? Would I ever be able to tell anyone? Would people know who I am? The more I uncovered, the more it became obvious that the months of therapy would become years.

Olivia encouraged me to build a support group of people who shared my beliefs and would not be judgmental. But she continued to tell me not to be quick in sharing my memories. "If they share with you, then you can begin to share with them. A little bit at a time. Go easy."

Once I opened myself up to building a support group, they seemed to come from everywhere. Previously unknown people suddenly stepped into my life to help me create a new world where I could heal. I wondered, as I often did when life seemed to open before me, if these people had always been there and I'd been unable to see them.

Wilderflowers, a plant and landscaping business specializing in flowers grown in southern Illinois, was five miles south of town, just off Highway 51 at the end of a gravel lane. I'd passed it every afternoon for years on my way home from work but never noticed it was there. Then one day, not long after Olivia began encouraging me to build my support group, I saw the small sign "Wilderflowers" leading to Jenny's shop. I'm uncertain as to why I turned down the lane. Maybe I was drawn out of curiosity, or maybe I was being led to meet someone I was destined to know.

Jenny had long blond hair, skin hardened by hours in the summer sun, and a spirit beaten down by a failed marriage. Her voice was a bit raspy, probably from years as a heavy smoker. But she had a gift, an uncanny way of talking to the flowers. She sometimes held a flower to her cheek and inhaled its fragrance as if the two of them were lovers. I soon became a regular customer and began hanging out with her and her co-worker. When business was slow, the three of us sat in lawn chairs strategically placed in the middle of flowers. Sometimes we enjoyed the silence of the day; other times, they taught me how to talk to the flowers. It took time and a willingness to explore my emotions with curiosity rather than judgment before I began to appreciate the beauty of a blooming coral bell. To hold the plants and experience the textures and colors each flower had to offer was remarkable.

One day, while looking through a landscaping magazine, I was drawn to the photograph of a dry creek that curled through the lawn like a giant snake. Berms covered by Mexican rocks and other stones of varying sizes and shapes flanked each end of the dry creek. Surrounding the bed was an assortment of flowering plants, ferns, hostas, and a small Japanese maple tree. The creative possibilities tested my imagination, and I wanted a dry creek of my own.

I showed the photo to Jenny. "You could do this!" she said, the pitch of her voice rising with enthusiasm. "Will there be lots of sun, or will it be more of a shade garden?" I outlined my plan for Jenny, who helped in my search for just the right plants.

I began working the next weekend. I dug out the creek bed and used the loose dirt to form berms on each end of the creek. Next, I lined the bed with landscaping plastic and gathered Mexican rocks and stones to cover the berms. Some of the rocks I could barely move. After placing each rock in a chosen place, I began planting: ostrich ferns, ornamental grasses, sedums, bronze fennel, and coral bell with their purple leaves and long stems that hold miniature white flowers. Occasionally I would stop to rub the soil between my fingers, breathe deeply, and let the earth speak to me. There, in the beauty of my dry creek, I felt as if I had staggered out of an emotional wilderness into a place where life had meaning. The dry creek became my laboratory, the place where my life began to change.

This work continued throughout the spring and summer. As the plants grew and my creation required additional plants, Jenny pointed out that if I wanted to bring living creatures to my creek bed, I would need to add a water source. So I placed a birdbath with a continuous flow of water in the middle of the creek, and it became a conduit for life. An earthworm crawled in and out of the loose dirt. Butterflies landed on my shoulder and the top of my head, and large bumble bees surrounded me as if we were friends. The occasional toad rested under a Japanese fern while chipmunks scampered about in their newly discovered world. The wind blew through the vegetation, and a wren sang a familiar lullaby. As I sat among my newly acquired friends, I considered all the people I'd found in my life since working with Olivia— Jenny at Wilderflowers, my yoga teacher Charlotte McCloud—who had made it possible for me to experience this beauty. I imagined them there, with the flowers. We sat together as if in a temple, where every word and thought is sacred, and I felt the presence of God.

INNER CHILD

2002
Makanda, Illinois

There's a belief in the mental health community that each of us carries a child deep within us. The child, who represents our childhood, is as we were many years ago. If our child was the beneficiary of a wholesome childhood, then we'll be the beneficiary of that positive influence in our adult life. If, on the other hand, the child was abused, then the adult will take on the symptoms of an abused child: lack of trust, inability to experience intimacy, low self-esteem. Only when we heal the inner child can we expect the adult to be free of a traumatic past.

Olivia reminded me that my past behavior was based, in part, on the physical and sexual abuse I had experienced. She encouraged me to focus on the present even as we dug into my past. "Larry, you have so many wonderful qualities," she said. "You are a very honest and compassionate man. Tell me what you were like while growing up on the farm. Tell me about that little boy, your inner child."

I reacted quickly. "I was disgusting, dirty, wore old, ragged clothes. A weakling. I should have stopped Keith."

Olivia leaned back in her chair and watched in silence. Several seconds passed. I felt ashamed. "I can't believe I just said those things about myself."

"Maybe you hold your inner child responsible for the abuse. That is a common reaction among abuse victims. But you were too small to stop your brother, who was six years older and much larger than you. There was nothing you could have done to stop him. Reach out and hold the hand of your inner child. Let him feel your love." Olivia reached over and held my hand. As we sat there in her small office while she held my hand, I was reminded of a day-care facility located across the street from my office. Each day one of the teachers took the children for a walk. Each child was connected to the teacher by a walking rope. It could be one or many children holding onto the rope. As Olivia held my hand, I imagined the two of us connected by an invisible walking rope, and she was trying to get my inner child to hold on so she could lead us both through the healing process.

She suggested I write a letter to my inner child. After a few attempts, I told her that I couldn't come up with anything, and the subject was dropped. Months later, she renewed her request, and once again, I was faced with the uncomfortable task of communicating with my inner child.

One evening, I was meditating in the lower level of our home when I imagined a middle-aged man, much like myself, wandering the countryside in search of something. The experience was similar to my meditations on the De Land farmhouse. It was as if I were looking down on this man from above. As I focused my attention on him, I noticed that he was physically fit, well-dressed, and appeared to enjoy the material trappings of happiness. But the longer I focused on him, the more I became aware of a relentless pain below his skin and bones. It was this pain that had sent him searching the countryside. He was looking for an antidote. During his search, he came upon a woman I had never seen. There was a quiet peace about her, and I felt confident that she could help him. As I concentrated on the man and the woman, she pointed to a tall mountain in the distance. She seemed to be telling the man he needed to go there. The terrain was rugged, and the man had no way to get there but to walk, but he nodded and began trekking in the direction of the mountain. I stayed with the man for a time, but the walk was long and there was nothing between him and the mountain, so I opened my eyes and left him.

Over the next few days, I revisited the man in my meditation. Each time, I found him trekking toward the mountain. Sometimes the land was dark and rocky, and other times it was light and pleasant. The mountain was always a little closer until one day, he was there. The mountain towered above him, but I could see a path leading up the mountain that looked primitive, but passable.

I shared my experience with Olivia at our next visit. "Who is this man?" she asked.

"I suppose it's me, but it doesn't feel like me. It's as if I'm watching someone else."

"Would you like to revisit this visualization?"

I considered her question. I was happy for any chance to put away the search for my inner child and explore something else. Was Olivia really suggesting we do that? Or did she think this middle-aged man was connected to my inner child in some way? The uncertainty was worrying but tantalizing. I agreed.

Olivia took my hand. "Close your eyes and visualize the man walking up the mountain. Walk with him."

I closed my eyes and concentrated on my breathing, secure in the light touch of Olivia's hand which kept me tethered and safe.

"What do you see?"

"The man is hiking up the mountain. He thinks at the top of the mountain he can find true happiness."

"Can he?"

"I'm not sure."

"Visualize him at the top of the mountain. What does he find there?"

I visualized the man reaching the top of the mountain. "It looks like a monastery that's grown out of the mountain. The buildings are small with walls of speckled granite. There are several men dressed in brown robes with sandals strapped to their feed. There are gardens filled with vegetation, donkeys, rabbits, dogs, and cows."

"Good. Let's go back to the men in sandals. Look closely. Do you recognize any of them?"

When I focused on the men of the monastery, I noticed that one of them sat under a large tree. He seemed to be deep in thought. He was a lean man, built like a long-distance runner with a freshly shaved head. When I looked closer, he opened his eyes, and a slight smile grew on his face. "Welcome, Larry," the lean man said. "I've been expecting you. Come, sit, and tell me of your pain."

I opened my eyes. My heart was beating rapidly, and I had cold sweats. Olivia slid the trash can toward me, and I threw up into it. When I told her what I'd seen, she nodded. "I want you to revisit this in your meditations, Larry. Let me know at our next visit if you see anything new. Will you do that?"

I did not want to, but I agreed. We did a few breathing exercises to end the session, and I went home.

That evening I threw up again and went to bed early.

The next day was a Wednesday. I still didn't feel well, but I wanted to keep my commitment to Olivia. I decided I would try revising the visualization with the man under the tree who I had begun calling "Father Ramero." That evening, I retreated to the lower level of my home, turned off all the lights except for the single nightlight in the wall, settled into my chair, and closed my eyes.

I can't be sure, but I don't think it was very long before I could see the man sitting under the tree with Father Ramero. They were meditating. I don't know how long they had been there, but it was darker than it had been before. I watched them a while, matching my breathing with theirs. Then the man opened his eyes. He seemed sad, but I didn't know why. I looked at Father Ramero and was shocked to see tears. The front of his robe was wet. Father Ramero spoke, "I saw a boy with a bent neck and a dog whose tail wouldn't wag. Your inner child is in a great deal of pain. Sit with your child, learn to know him, learn to love him. You're welcome to stay with us for the duration of your journey."

During my next session, I told Olivia about my visualization, that I had not been feeling well, and that I didn't know what had caused the problem. I asked her if the work I had been doing on my inner child was the reason.

"I'm feeling overly stressed and don't know why."

"Is that what you want to talk about?"

"Yes, we need to visit my inner child. But it's difficult work."

"Yes, I know it is."

I looked slightly down to the floor, closed my eyes.

"What do you see?" Olivia asked.

"I see the man. He's meditating. He's trying to find his inner child."

"See if you can see what the man sees." She gave my hand a light squeeze. "Take it slow, Larry. I'm right here."

I focused on the man and put all my energy into seeing what he saw behind his closed eyes. Finally, it happened. I don't know how it happened, but it did, and I knew immediately why Father Ramero had been so upset when they first sat together. I saw the little boy standing in a dusty road. The light was dim. He was close to seven years of age. He wore a cap made of brown vinyl, cracked and peeled from the sun. His shoes were scuffed, and his faded flannel shirt hung lower on the left side because it had not been buttoned properly. But this was not what had made Father Ramero so upset. What had made Father Ramero weep was that the boy could not lift his head. His neck was bent at a forty-five-degree angle. I thought he was looking at the ground, but when he tried to make eye contact with me, he couldn't lift his head. He struggled to move his neck, but the muscles had atrophied from years of not looking up, and now he couldn't. Leaning against the child's leg was a solemn dog that continually looked up at the boy's face. Like the boy's neck, the dog's tail could not move. This was the dog whose tail wouldn't wag.

I lay on the ground to get into a position to make eye contact with the boy. We struggled, and eventually, the boy with the bent neck and I were able to look at each other but only as strangers. In disappointment, I opened my eyes and told Olivia what I had seen.

"Larry, do you love your little boy?" Olivia asked.

Silence. Then I said, "I'm not sure. I know that I should. But I've tried to forget him. He is sad and evil. If I get too close to him, will I feel his pain? I don't know if I could handle it."

Olivia nodded. "I understand that this is hard for you. Consider all the progress you made today, Larry. Will you continue working on this at home?"

With some hesitation, I agreed.

That night, I had a dream. In my dream, I was sitting with Father Ramero under the tree. I told him of my life and a childhood squandered by physical and sexual abuse. Father Ramero asked me if I trusted him, and I said yes. "Larry, let's hold on to each other for a while. I want you to feel the love I have for you. There's nothing dangerous or abusive about it. I expect nothing in return. It's my hope and expectation that you will view my love as the presence of God."

I agreed, and we embraced for a very long time.

"I love you," I said.

"And I love you," Father Ramero answered. "Go and be with your child."

Then, in my dream, I was no longer with Father Ramero, but I was with the boy. The child and I stood at my dry creek surrounded by an assortment of flowers and ornamental grasses. The boy seemed to be in his natural habitat as he quickly knelt, dug into the dirt, and gently held two ladybugs and a fishing worm that moved slowly across his hand. Next, he transferred the worm to my hand while the two of us watched and wondered if it was a boy or girl. As the inner child leaned downward, the worm slid into the freshly dug soil.

Without conversation, my inner child led me deep into the heart of a cornfield next to the farmhouse. We stopped at a low-lying area, some twenty feet in circumference, where the water had stunted the corn's growth.

There was room for the two of us and my dog to sit and watch the golden cornstalks bend in the direction of the wind. For the moment, we sat in peace and watched a dragonfly dive toward a mud-hole filled by recent rain. The dragonfly skimmed the water's surface, allowing his belly to touch the water. My inner child rose to his feet and struggled to walk. Surprised, I asked what was wrong. The child unbuckled his pants and showed me his backside. I could see fresh blood running down the back of his legs. I knew what had happened. Suddenly, I was a wild animal in pursuit, tearing a three-foot path through the cornfield toward the farmhouse. I felt the sting of the stalks on my skin, and the boy experienced the slashing of the corn silk across his forearm and face. My mind was bent on killing Keith for raping my inner child, and I was prepared to kill my mother and father for allowing it to happen. My mouth bellowed the wailing sounds of a wild animal looking for the kill. When I found them, I ripped the flesh from their bones with my fingers and left their shredded, blood-covered body parts laying about.

I woke, shaking from the rage I had felt in my dream. It felt as if an accumulation of decades-long anger had exploded throughout my body. Bile rising in my throat, I raced to the bathroom, leaned over the toilet, and began to gag.

When I returned to bed, Paula shifted in the darkness. "Larry, what's wrong?"

I lay in bed, unable to close my eyes, and struggled to tell her what I had seen. She comforted me, her soft voice in the dark soothing my anger until I was able to concentrate on my breathing and drift back to sleep.

Over the next few sessions, Olivia encouraged me to return to the image of the boy with the bent neck and a dog whose tail wouldn't wag. I imagined the two of us at my dry creek, sitting in quiet meditation. From there we began holding hands and becoming familiar with the touch of our skin. I apologized to the boy for my neglectful ways. I wanted to make things right, but the boy refused to speak. So I asked him about his past, about the abuse he endured, and then the boy began to speak. The boy told of a life with an older brother who beat him, raped him, and walked with evil in his eyes. He told of being held by his ankles, dangled out the window of the hayloft, and warned that he would be dropped if he revealed such horrors. He told of a father who, when he divorced his wife, kept his older son and sent Larry to live with his mother. The boy's emotional pain felt like raw flesh burning in the summer sun.

As the boy told his story, the lines running from the dog's eyes to his nose became wet from a steady flow of tears. Moved by the story, I picked up the little boy and his dog, placed both on my lap, and held them for hours. Tears flowed down my face and dropped onto the little boy and his dog. Then something magical happened. The boy's neck began to move. He looked up into my eyes and said, "I love you."

"And I love you," I said. The boy's face took on a smile, and that's when the dog's tail began to wag.

PHOTOS

Wendall Franklin and Larry Franklin
milking cow at the farm near De Land, Illinois, 1944.

Franklin Brothers:
Woodrow, James, Wendall, Paul, Henry
at De Land, Illinois, 1940s.

Larry Franklin and Keith Franklin,
De Land, Illinois, 1947.

Larry Franklin, second grade,
Grandmother Tolliver's porch in Louisville, Illinois, 1950.

Wendall B. Franklin and C. Gatha Franklin
on front porch of farm house, De Land, Illinois, 1940.

Larry Franklin and Keith Franklin,
personal photo, 1949.

Artist's rendering of a photograph taken of the wreckage
of the car, shortly after Wendall Franklin's car accident.
Mt. Pulaski, Illinois, August 18, 1950.

The watch worn by Wendall Franklin
at the time of his car accident.

Franklin farmhouse and barn, De Land, Illinois, 1950.

Photo of Dry Creek, Makanda, Illinois, 2006.

A cornfield located near De Land, Illinois—
Larry Franklin's sanctuary from sexual abuse.

PART III
THE HEALING

You Can't Know
What You Don't Know

1995
Makanda, Illinois

Photographs show the brain as approximately the size of a grapefruit and looking like a large, pinkish-gray walnut. It grows not unlike the rest of our body, weighing about one pound at birth, two pounds at early childhood, and three pounds as an adult.

According to scientist Bessel van der Kolk, the amygdala is the emotional and instinctual center. The hippocampus controls memory, and the prefrontal cortex is responsible for regulating emotions and impulses. All three work together to manage stress. These are the parts of the brain most likely to be affected by trauma.

When traumatic experiences surface, the amygdala goes into overdrive, acting as it would if you were experiencing the trauma for the first time. The prefrontal cortex also becomes suppressed, so you're less capable of controlling your fear, leaving you in a purely reactive state. Meanwhile, trauma leads to reduced activity in the hippocampus, one function of which is to distinguish between past and present. In other words, your brain can't tell the difference between the actual traumatic event and the memory of it. It perceives things that trigger memories of traumatic events as threats themselves.

In a 1999 article published in *Current Opinion in Pediatrics,* Dr. Bruce Perry, senior fellow at the Child Trauma Academy in Houston, explains that when a child experiences "excess activation of the neural systems" from exposure to violence, this can impact the "emotional, behavioral and cognitive functioning" of the child in fundamental ways."*

When a traumatic event threatens someone, they will react with a "fight" or "flight" response. But children, because of their small stature, are unable to fight or escape from their perpetrator. They may look to a caretaker, but if no such person exists, the child is left to other means. Children exposed to chronic violence might report a variety of dissociative experiences—going to an imaginary place, feeling numb, or just floating—all classic symptoms.

I had used dissociation to remove myself from the physical and sexual abuse. It was my coping mechanism that allowed me to survive. I became convinced that dissociation had also affected cognitive function impeding my ability to learn. Perry believes that a child

* Perry, B. D., and Azad, I. (1999). Post-traumatic stress disorders in children and adolescents. *Current Opinion in Pediatrics.* 2:121–132.

exposed to physical and sexual abuse functioned differently than one raised in a safe environment. While my learning problems began in childhood, they carried over into adulthood.

Some of my most frustrating moments were as a college student when I attended lectures, hoping to retain bits of intellectual thought. The stakes were high. I attended the University of Illinois, a place that graduates scholars, a place where failure means expulsion, and a trip back to your hometown where people will mock you for your pathetic performance. Reading the textbook was equally frustrating. I ended each meaningless paragraph with an empty mind, unable to process information. I tried everything—listening intently, watching the movement of the instructor's lips, taking notes, and praying that I would understand. I would not accept that I was intellectually incapable.

I began by reading a single sentence and refused to move on until I understood each word. Then, and only then, would I move to the next sentence, and then the next, the next, and the next, until I understood the complete paragraph. The process was slow, tedious, and brought an occasional scream from my mouth. I often ran to the nearest bar where I drank, waiting for death to tap my shoulder and ask if I was ready to pass. Even with my low level of comprehension, I managed to secure my bachelor's and master's degrees, a remarkable feat.

Human beings, miraculous in every detail, have an astonishing ability to endure the most horrendous experiences. When I was physically and sexually abused, my mind took me to another place, numbed my feelings, fragmented my thoughts, and kept me from dying. As an adult, the childhood abuse, never fully digested, attracted me more to death than life.

But human beings are incredibly adaptive creatures. After years of therapy, my image of life cleared. My mind woke, crisp and agile. I began to enjoy reading books, attending lectures, or having an engaging, intellectual conversation with a stranger at the local coffee shop. Learning, which had eluded me for decades, was now a continuous gift. My support system, a gift from God, also continued to grow. I could be with friends as if we were in a temple where every word and thought was sacred; I could freely share gentle hugs while sharing my friends' happiness and sitting with their pain, and I could share my love with the glance of an eye or the touch of a hand.

Gone was the wild animal in the cornfield.

Gone was the boy with the bent neck and a dog whose tail wouldn't wag.

IN THE BACKSEAT OF MY 1955 FORD

1960–1965
Louisville, Illinois

It was late on a Saturday evening in July 1960, and a group of us were hanging outside the local skating rink and drinking a few beers. Three of the girls were from Flora, Illinois, a small town seven miles south of Louisville. One of the girls was blond-haired, sixteen-year-old Sarah. She had a reputation among my friends for being open to "affectionate activities." The combination of me having drunk a few beers and Sarah's reputation convinced me to ask if I could drive her home. She was agreeable. Before we left the group, my friend handed me a condom.

"Be safe," he said as I tucked the condom into my pocket.

As Sarah and I drove down the winding country roads, our intentions were clear. Sarah wanted to find love in the backseat of my 1955 Ford, and I wanted to lose my virginity. I found a secluded spot next to a mature cornfield and parked the car.

It was a clear night, and the moon was full. After a few kisses, we opened the doors and moved to the back seat, where empty beer cans laid on the floorboard of my car. Sarah and I helped undress each other. The night brought a light breeze that cooled our backsides. I pulled the condom from the pocket of my jeans. Everything was perfect; I was going to lose my virginity.

Sarah lay naked on the back seat. Her large blue eyes seemed to look through me, and her lips were seductively heavy. She told me she was having her period. I told her not to worry. Everything will be fine. I leaned over her, the condom in my hand. I paused to look down and study her body. I was surprised by how familiar she looked, as if I had been with her many times before. I felt a distance that was offset by our closeness. As I saw her pubic hair, I knew something was wrong. My brain froze as if I had pressed the pause button on a video. I struggled to make sense of the situation. I felt trapped in an endless maze, not knowing which way to go. Danger emanated from somewhere nearby, and I felt as if I were about to die. I did the only thing that I could do: dress and get away.

I didn't speak. Neither did Sarah. We moved to the front seat and began the thirty-minute trip to her home. The only sound was the tires wrestling the country roads and the evening breeze blowing through the open windows. We pulled up to her house. Sarah stepped out of the car and ran across the grass to her front door. My foot eased up on the clutch, and I dove away.

I traveled to an isolated spot and drank well into the early morning. I was a failure. Men were supposed to have sex with women. They were programmed for this moment. It was part of their DNA. *What is wrong with me?* I replayed the scene in my mind over and over. *Something went wrong when I looked down at her and saw her pubic hair.* It didn't make any sense. I had wanted to have sex with Sarah. So why wasn't I able to? I thought that if my dad and brother were alive, they would have unloaded profanity and a beating on me.

I looked for an excuse and blamed the beer. I'd drunk too much beer. That's why I couldn't perform. To think otherwise meant that I could not function as a man. Yes, it had to be the beer.

Three months later, I met a single mom who I will call Jan. She was a few years older than me, a woman who had sexual experience and could help me find my way. And yes, Jan liked to drink beer as well. The two of us had gone out on a couple of dates. Although I had met her daughter, a precious five-year-old with long, dark hair, I did not allow this purity to distract me from my objective of having sex with her mother.

Jan was an attractive woman with a body that the stress of childbirth had not diminished. Her dark hair and deep, green eyes gave her a mysterious, quiet, and radiant look. This was our third date. Sex was imminent. After a few beers at a bowling alley just north of Louisville, the two of us traveled the country roads, searching for a suitable spot to park. I'd had only two beers, so I was confident I should perform without any problems.

There, just down the road, was a bare cornfield with a dirt road hugging its western border. The corn had been picked, leaving darkness as our only shield. *This will do*, I thought. The two of us parked, moved to the backseat, and drank another beer. As before, there was no foreplay. I was on a mission to have sex with Jan. We removed our clothes and draped them across the front seat. As before, I looked at her body and saw her pubic hair. As before, everything went wrong. My mind froze, and I momentarily forgot why I was in the backseat. I sat there, a shell of a boy, until I did the only thing I could do—dress and get away. I pulled my pants off the front seat and began to dress. Jan followed my cue, and the two of us dressed in silence. We moved to the front seat, and I drove her home. Although we never spoke, her anger filled the car like a heavy fog—dark, thick, and relentlessly depressive.

My attempts at a normal sex life came to a halt. I decided to focus my time on becoming the best trumpet player I could become and bury any thoughts of having sex. Hours and hours of practice, and a love for music, helped me develop into an excellent high school trumpet player. But that was not enough. I wanted to become a professional musician. While at the University of Illinois, I would practice and drink beer. As the years passed, I became good at both.

During my four years at the university, I never asked a woman out for a date. This is not to say that there weren't times when I wanted to, but the fear of repeating my experience with Sarah and Jan kept me focused on what I was supposed to do: practice my trumpet and drink beer.

After graduating from the University of Illinois, I went to Southern Illinois University to work on a master's degree in music. I was granted an assistantship to teach trumpet to undergraduates and to perform in various ensembles. My plan to be a professional musician was going well, and I was keeping away from women. Until Sheila.

Sheila was an undergraduate music student who came to a club where I performed in a small jazz group. She was an attractive woman who drew my attention. She had long, wavy, blond hair that moved across her face when she turned her head and looked my way. She had blue eyes, a light tan, and a slightly sad expression until she decided to smile. It was quite seductive. She was sitting alone at a table close to the bandstand. It felt obvious that she was there to see me.

After the group stopped playing, I walked up to Sheila and asked if I could join her. After she nodded yes, I took a seat across the table from her. We had a brief conversation before she had to check in at her dormitory by midnight. It was the campus rules in those days. I asked if I could walk her back to the dorm. Upon reaching the dormitory, a few kisses quickly turned into something more passionate. The motivation was strong enough that I wanted to spend more time with her. We agreed upon a date for the following Saturday. As I left Sheila that night, memories of Sarah and Jan returned. I couldn't help but wonder if this was a mistake.

We arranged to meet at my apartment Saturday evening. So even though the storyline was familiar—a desperate virgin hoping to sleep with a beautiful woman who liked to drink beer and shared a mutual goal to have sex—I hoped the change in setting would change the ending. Maybe the backseat of a 1955 Ford had been the problem.

As before, there was no foreplay. The two of us undressed. Sheila lay down on my bed, and I moved on top of her. I wanted this. I looked down at her naked body, and as soon as I saw her pubic hair, I lost all direction. All cognitive skills were gone. I was a shell of a man.

I stood up. I began to dress. Sheila sat up and followed my cue. I don't know who finished first. Neither of us spoke.

We left my apartment, and I drove her to her dormitory. The silence was smothering. I could feel the depression grab hold of my body and pull at my last breath. When I pulled up to Sheila's dorm, I had barely stopped the car before she opened the passenger door and ran inside. Shame and guilt overwhelmed me. There was something wrong with me, and I didn't know what to do.

I saw Sheila on campus a few times, but I was too embarrassed to talk with her. We never spoke again.

I relived the experience through my mind over and over. The attraction to Sheila was strong, and I wanted to be with her. I could not understand what was wrong with me. Still, I somehow managed to move past my failure and direct my sight on the original goal: practice my trumpet and drink beer.

For the rest of my time at Southern Illinois University, I avoided any contact with women and focused on completing my master's degree. After I received my degree, I began to wonder if whatever was wrong with my mind would allow me to take a break and be with a woman. I knew that something was wrong with me, but the idea of seeing a psychologist did not cross my mind. I didn't believe anyone had answers to why I was still a virgin.

As an accomplished musician, I had been offered a contract to become a full-time faculty member of the music school at Southern Illinois University. After I signed, my boss, the Assistant Dean for the College of Fine Arts, and I talked about what my plans might be. As we talked, a beautiful woman stood up from her desk and walked across the room.

My boss noticed me looking at her. "She's a student worker at the university." Then he said jokingly, motioning toward the student-worker, "Now that you have your bachelor's and master's degrees and full-time employment at the university, maybe it's time for you to think about marriage."

I laughed. "Maybe you have a point. She does look good. What's her name?"

"Paula."

I did like the way Paula walked across the floor, but once my boss and I ended our conversation, I moved on to practice my trumpet and drink some beer.

A few weeks later, a friend and I went to a local bar for a few drinks. It was a broken-down, smoke-filled place but large enough for a dance floor. I remember the beer was cold and tasted unusually good. I also remember my eyes being drawn to the dance floor and seeing Paula, the student-worker employed by my boss, the one who had looked good walking across the office floor. In those days, women didn't go to bars alone, so I knew the man she was dancing with was her date. I watched her over my friend's shoulder as she and her date danced most of the evening, returning to their table between songs to take sips from their beers.

Paula had some sensuous moves that won my attention. As my friend and I talked, I continued glancing over his shoulder, wrestling with the idea of asking her out. When Paula's date went to the restroom, I quickly walked to her table. Knowing her date would return soon, I needed to act quickly. After exchanging a few words, I asked her if she would like to go out with me sometime for drinks. Without hesitation, she agreed to see me next Saturday evening. I said great and rushed back to my table before her date returned.

The following Saturday, I picked up Paula around 8:00 pm. I was determined that this time would be different from my past experiences, so I committed to taking it nice and easy. No sex. I would get to know her. I would let myself be with the moment.

For our first date, I took her to a quiet bar frequented by graduate students and faculty—a great place for intellectual exchange or intimate conversations. Paula wore a tight sweater and form-fitting white jeans. Her long, brown hair draped over her shoulders. She was beautiful.

Even better, conversation was easy for us, and since I had no hidden agenda, I could enjoy myself without feeling it necessary for us to have sex.

After a few hours of talking and drinking, we left the bar. Paula sat in the middle of the seat as we drove back to her apartment. We walked to her front door, where we exchanged several passion-filled kisses, more intense than I had expected. It was enough for me to ask her for another date, another date, and many more.

On each date, the passion increased, and the intimacy deepened. I was taken with her. I began to care for her. *Are we becoming friends?* I wondered. *Is this what people call a relationship?* It felt a bit spiritual, like man's first glimpse of a sunrise.

Over time, the sexual experimentations led to sexual intercourse. It was like the two of us found our way together. One year later, we were married on a warm summer day in June 1967. Fifty-four years later and it has been more beautiful than anything I had imagined when I was with the women in the backseat of my 1955 Ford.

For years, I dealt with the shame of those experiences in the backseat of my car, not only for me but for the women who might have been emotionally hurt. Maybe they wondered if my behavior had been their fault. Or did they consider me a loser and move on? If I knew where to find them, I would want to explain my behavior and apologize if I caused them any pain.

"How could I have done such things?" I asked Olivia one day.

"You don't know what you don't know."

This caused me to lean back in my chair and think. When I asked Olivia such things, she had a way of forcing me to answer my own question. She thought it best if I figured it out. For me, this meant looking inward.

I sat there quietly for a moment, then I asked, "Do you think this has anything to do with the feelings I experience when making love?"

"Perhaps," Olivia said. "Tell me what you mean."

I told her how I sometimes felt anxiety when Paula and I made love, particularly at the beginning.

"Is this recent?"

"Yes, recently the feeling has become more intense. But I'm certain it's visited me at times throughout my life. I responded by forgetting about it. Sometimes with success. Other times, not so much."

"We need to find out where those feelings are coming from. Why don't you relax, close your eyes, and concentrate on your breathing?" I knew the routine, and in no time, I was relaxed.

"Larry, imagine that you are about to make love, and the anxiety is building."

My breathing accelerated. Seemingly from nowhere, I visualized walking down a rocky path until I saw the entrance to a cave.

"Larry, tell me what you see."

"It feels like I walked into a cave. I'm standing at the entrance, afraid to go in."

"Go ahead and walk in. You're safe. Nothing will hurt you."

I inched forward. My body began to shake, and a cold sweat covered me.

"Tell me what you see," Olivia said.

"I'm in the cave. It's dark, damp, and has the smell of mold. Ridges cover the walls. The walls are closing in, ready to suffocate me. Oh, my God. It's not a cave. It's a vagina." Stunned, I opened my eyes and shook my head in disbelief. "I can't believe what I saw. The cave, it's my mother's vagina."

Olivia didn't hesitate. "Let's go back to that image and try something. Put yourself back inside the dark cave, your mother's vagina. This time I want you to take both hands and push the walls away from you."

In a few seconds, I visualized the cave and felt the damp, rigid walls closing in on me. With a firm voice, Oliva said, "Take both arms and push the walls away from you."

As I pushed with both arms, I was shocked by how easily the walls moved away. The relief was immediate. I opened my eyes. "I can't believe how easy that was and how good it felt. I just pushed my mother out of my bedroom."

I couldn't help but laugh. "I feel like I just watched a low-budget sci-fi movie where some scary creature terrorized the world. It's like I have spent my entire life being chased by my mother's vagina." Both Olivia and I laughed about the image of a giant vagina chasing me around the countryside. Then the laughing subsided. There was silence. A broad smile, beaming with the satisfaction that I had made a major breakthrough, moved across Olivia's face. No words were needed.

For the next several weeks, I prefaced lovemaking with my wife by visualizing myself standing inside a giant vagina and pushing the walls away from myself. Each time, anxiety lessened, and my sexual performance improved. I made love with newfound confidence. Keith and my mother were no longer strapped to my back.

THE WHISKEY BARREL PIT

2000s
Olivia's Office

The journey I took to understand myself, past and present, was slow and required traversing varied terrain. Sometimes the path was direct and clear, such as when I examined recollections where abuse always left its tracks. Other times I fumbled in the darkness, unsure if I was even pointed in the right direction. At times like these, my subconscious found ways to nudge me in the right direction, usually in metaphors while I slept.

Two of the most vivid dreams featured sewage.

The sky was overcast, as in most dreams, and it was unusually quiet. In my backyard was a large hole—six feet deep and wide enough for an average-size man to stand—that exposed a rust-colored, clay sewer pipe. The top of the pipe was broken off, creating an opening with rough edges that resembled torn flesh. Rushing through the pipe was a stream of sewage that ran horizontally and then dropped off and disappeared. For hours, I watched the endless flow of liquid that appeared to have originated from our house some thirty feet away.

I woke. And as I always did after dreaming, I lay in bed searching for meaning. This time, it didn't take long. I had taken my childhood pain and shoved it down my throat, never allowing it to surface. If I let it out, I might die. The pipe represented my throat. The sewage was my pain. The house mirrored my body.

A few days after the dream about the sewer pipe, I found myself in another dream that took place in my backyard. An open pit, ten feet from side to side, held what appeared to be the bottom half of a whiskey barrel. It was constructed with wood a thickness of one-half inch and buried, so the top edge stood a few inches above the ground. The pit was filled with a dark slurry that swirled rapidly in a counter-clockwise motion, creating a funnel-like effect, dragging everything down to the unknown.

While I felt an irresistible urge to enter the pit, my legs locked up, and my body shook. I needed a plan. I would pull my pickup truck to the edge of the pit and attach one end of a thick rope to my waist and the other end to the truck's bumper. As a precaution, I would ask Olivia to sit in my truck and pull me out if I lost control and began to go under. Even so, I could not enter the pit.

At my next session, I told Olivia about my dream and how I could not enter the water. She agreed that it was a powerful dream and one that we might explore. She suggested I close my eyes and visualize the open pit. In seconds, I visualized the water swirling in a counter-clockwise motion.

With the rope attached to my waist and to the bumper, I stood at the edge. As part of my visualization,

Olivia sat in the truck and assured me that I would be safe. She backed the truck until the rope became taut. I stepped into the water and gripped the edge of the pit with both hands. Each time I tried to move, my body stiffened.

"Larry, let the image go."

I slowly opened my eyes.

"You appear to be on the edge of a panic attack. Were you able to move away from the edge?" she asked.

I shook my head.

"Let's try something a little different. This time when you visualize the pit, make it big like a swimming pool, so the current is away from the edge."

I closed my eyes and focused on my breathing. Soon I saw a much larger pit with rough water in the middle and calm water along the edge. With a depth of four feet and a flat bottom that extended five feet from the side, I felt secure. As I moved away from the edge, the bottom plunged to an unknown depth, forcing me to swim if I continued. For the moment, I stayed in the shallow water. Then the water changed, taking on the appearance of stew. But unlike stew with its customary carrots, potatoes, chopped celery, and pieces of beef, this stew was filled with memories. In front of me, my father's decapitated body bobbed up and down like a fishing cork. In his right hand, he cradled his head covered in sadness, eyes hidden by swollen lids. To my left, an erect penis moved across the water's surface like a submarine's periscope. Everywhere I looked, my mother's body floated and then disappeared, only to resurface somewhere else. Suddenly, where my dad's body had been, Keith's seaweed-covered cadaver rose above the surface like a killer whale coming up for air and disappeared back into the stew.

"Larry, tell me what you see."

I told her about my dad's body, the erect penis, and Keith floating in the stew around me.

"Your dream and today's visualization exercise are warning you that buried feelings don't stay buried."

"Yes, the object is to sit with my demons, my bad memories, and in time the anxiety will decrease. What feels horrific now will become like a distant memory."

"Precisely. Instead of burying your feelings so you can relive traumatic events on a cognitive level and protect yourself from the pain, it would help if you meditated and spent some time being with the bad memories."

Olivia paused as if waiting for a response. I didn't have one because I knew she was right. I just nodded.

She continued, "Larry, try to visualize the pit, but this time I want you to concentrate on your breathing and feeling relaxed. Just be present with the objects floating in the stew. I promise you will be safe."

In seconds, I was in the swirling stew. This time I focused on my breathing and tried to be with the images. Various objects—my parents' bodies and Keith's corpse and the erect penis—brushed against my legs as I moved through the shallow water. At first, I flinched, but I soon was able to stand firm and experience only slight anxiety from memories associated with each object. My hands were still clenched, but my body and my breathing remained steady. After a few minutes, Olivia released me from the visualization and congratulated me on my progress. It was time to unwind the session and move myself to the dry creek, the place where peace was welcome.

At my next session a week later, Olivia ushered me into her office with her familiar "Come on in, Larry, and have a seat. What would you like to work on today?"

I settled into the loveseat, and as was my habit, I checked the wastepaper basket next to the sofa. It was full. Must have been a bad day. I looked up to see Olivia watching me. "Are you really asking me what I would like to work on or what I need to work on? Because they're not the same thing, you know."

She laughed, "Good point, Larry. Let me rephrase the question: What do you need to work on today?" Her eyes smiled as she asked, but behind the smile was resolve as powerful as my fear. We'd been doing this for too long for me to pretend I didn't know the answer to that question.

"Well, I suppose I should work on the pit of stew. It certainly brings up a lot of issues." That was an understatement.

"Yes, I agree," Olivia replied briskly. "That would be a good place to start." Her voice softened a bit, and she said, "Maybe you could venture out into the deeper water this time. Sit back, relax, and concentrate on your breathing."

I leaned back, closed my eyes, and concentrated on each breath. In . . . out . . . in . . . out . . . My shoulders dropped, the tension left my arms, and then my entire body began to relax. The image of the open pit became clear: calm waters along the edge, turbulent waters in the center. The memories were all present: my naked mother, my decapitated father, my scary brother, and the erect penis that moved across the water's surface.

I described the images to Olivia, so she would know where I was and what I was seeing, then I moved past the shallow water and began to swim. The currents drew me to the center, where I disappeared below the surface and was pulled downward until I reached the bottom. I pushed my feet against the floor of the pit and bounced back to the surface. I was in the shallows again. I had survived.

I was surprised there had been a bottom and that I was still alive. This encouraged me to move to the middle. Again, I was dragged to the bottom and bounced back to the surface. This time, I saw that the current had moved my father close to me. His lower body was still submerged, while his decapitated torso bobbed like a cork in the water; his head was still cradled in the crook of his right arm. I took the head and placed it on top of his body. I rubbed the neck like I was working with putty. The more I rubbed, the more the severed head connected to my dad's body. He was facing me, so I saw the moment his eyes opened. His face looked sad, but he was alive. We hugged.

Olivia must have noticed a change in my demeanor because I heard her asking me, "Larry, what do you see?" I opened my eyes and smiled. "I hugged Dad, and it felt good."

September 10, 2014

Makanda, Illinois

As a child, whatever I knew about love came from my dog, Nippy. Whether I was running through the pasture jumping over cow piles, walking the bean rows, or hiding in the cornfields, Nippy was by my side. I sometimes tested his affection by lying on the floor next to a bowl filled with dog food covered with yesterday's gravy. I moved close to the bowl as his coarse white hair rubbed against my cheek. While pretending to eat his food, I was surprised by his passive behavior and lack of hostility. Only when I made a growling sound did Nippy show his teeth.

Dr. Bruce Perry, who studies the behaviors of child abuse victims, noted that many abused children found more "nurturing, predictable and unconditional experiences" with animals than with the "unpredictable adults" in their lives.*

---

* Perry, B. D., & Szalavitz, M. (2017). *The Boy Who Was Raised as a Dog: And Other Stories from a Child Psychiatrist's Notebook—What Traumatized Children Can Teach Us about Loss, Love, and Healing* (3rd ed.). Basic Books.

My childhood mind fantasized about being raised by a family of dogs in which the adult dogs were my parents, and the puppies were my siblings. While the adult dogs provided protection, the puppies offered fearless play. I marveled at how all inhabitants of the animal world formed families that were filled with love and compassion, unlike anything I had experienced.

Decades later, when I was well into therapy, I asked Olivia why I was unable to feel. "What is wrong with me? I see others who hold on to sadness when tragedy strikes. But I'm unable to feel it." She reminded me that because of my abusive childhood, I had blocked my feelings in order to survive. She promised me that in time, I would experience happiness and sadness like I'd never felt before.

Learning to feel was not sudden and magical. It was a long emotional journey that evolved into a spiritual path I follow to this day. But the trip was not without risk. Unwittingly, I had spent the last forty-five years of my life in an endless emotional wilderness, unaware of the childhood abuses I carried. Ironically, there had been safety walking in my darkness. I was an empty soul but didn't know it. Now that the shadows had lifted, and I could see the desert I walked and the burdens I carried, I needed to find my way out. Otherwise, I'd be trapped without the protection of ignorance. What sort of creatures might I see then? Would they suck my soul dry? Who would I become?

To escape who I was, a level of desperation was needed, a willingness to see the unseen, and a psychotherapist who served as my companion into the unknown. Olivia did not navigate the journey. She was an advisor who helped me make sense of the unknown and navigate a treacherous road. I trusted her, and that allowed me to take the journey slow and easy, like a summer rain.

When I was a university music student, it was a common belief among musicians that you fall into one of two categories: those who perform with feeling and those who are mere mechanics. I always considered myself to be the former, a trumpet player who played with feeling. But now, decades later, I realize that I had barely touched my emotional depth. Today, if I were still playing the trumpet, I can only imagine the intensity of emotion I would experience.

Music is a play between tension and release. A musical phrase is composed of a collection of notes— sixteenths, eighths, quarters, halves, and others with different durations—separated by time, commonly called rests. The musician, given a level of expertise, shapes the phrase by adding vibrato, a hesitation here or there, maybe a slight bending of the note, a tone as clear as light, or raspy as a voice in pain. The phrase can be long, demanding a full breath, or only a note or two for effect. These, too, give the music its movement, its flow. Throughout the phrase, the tension builds to a climax, requiring a cadence to set up the release. Depending on the strength of the tension and the expertise of the musician, the release can be quite powerful as you prepare for an emotional landing.

Artists have always pursued emotional intensities, and sometimes, when their art alone couldn't satisfy them, they turned to drugs as a conduit for emotion. As a teenager, alcohol was my drug of choice. The buzz from a six-pack of beer allowed me to flirt with ecstasy. As a man, dogs were my conduit for compassion and a reminder that death was a cadence, the period before another phrase begins, not the sudden and cold violence I had known. Some people who know me have said that I love dogs more than humans. While they're not wrong, it was a fawn-colored boxer named PJ who taught me that death is part of a greater rhythm, the passing of one life to another. She contributed to my well-being more than any other dog I've had.

Shelley, my youngest daughter, and I wanted a new puppy after our previous dog had died. We had been reading books on a variety of dogs, and one of them described Boxers as "Highly intelligent, easily trainable, and good with children." I knew they were also an active breed, but since Shelley was thirteen and I was in my early forties, we figured we could handle a Boxer. It was a Sunday afternoon when we purchased PJ. On the way home, I remembered that I was supposed to buy a gallon of milk. I pulled into a nearby grocery store and told Shelley to stay with PJ while I picked up some milk. As I got out of the car, a young couple with a full-grown Boxer parked next to me. I waited until one of them stepped out of the car and asked them if that was their Boxer. I pointed to Shelley in the back seat, holding a squirming PJ in her lap, and told them we'd just purchased a Boxer puppy.

"How do you like your dog?" I asked.

"We love her, but she's a bit crazy."

"What do you mean?" Their remark got my attention.

The wife started laughing, and the husband explained. "One day, our two-year-old Boxer was standing inside the living room of our house while we were outside with the neighbors. There was a large picture window separating us from our dog. You need to understand that Boxers are *people dogs*. They always want to be with people. Our dog backed up and took a running leap through the glass picture window to join us."

"Oh no, was she hurt?"

The man smiled and moved toward the grocery store, "No, not at all," he said with a wave. "Enjoy your new Boxer."

Several months later, we began having our own experiences with PJ. I had built a large, five-foot-tall farmer's fence that we called the Boxer Corral. It seemed the ideal solution for letting PJ stay outside while we were at work and the girls were in school. The first day after completing the Boxer Corral, we came home and found PJ had somehow escaped and was checking out the neighborhood. I saw no way PJ could have escaped from the corral, so the next morning, after Paula had gone to work and the kids to school, I hid in the house to see if I could catch her escaping. At first, she just walked around the corral, but after a few minutes, she grabbed hold of the fence and pulled herself over the side. I immediately went to Dillinger's Feed Store and purchased a battery and a roll of wire to attach to the fence. The line of electric wire ensured that this was the last time she ever climbed over the fence.

More than a decade had passed and PJ was thirteen-years-old. She had lost ten pounds and her appetite. Her hips had deteriorated to the point where she experienced difficulty walking up and down stairs. Since the life expectancy for Boxers is ten to twelve years, PJ's declining health was not a surprise. But she was more than a pet to fetch a ball or take orders to sit or to stay; she was a partner in a relationship where feelings were transferred by the touch of a hand or the glance of an eye rather than the clumsiness of the spoken word. I loved PJ and wanted her to have a good quality of life. But as her health declined, I had to make a choice. Should I have her put down? I didn't want to lose my best friend.

I went to our family veterinarian, Dr. Greenwell, a young vet who had the expertise and love that I wanted for PJ. As Greenwell entered the room, PJ looked up and slowly wagged her tail, not the rapid-moving tail we were used to. Still, the slow wag of her tail showed that PJ loved Dr. Greenwell.

"There's been a rapid decline in PJ's health," I said. "She's experienced a sudden weight loss. I don't want to put her to sleep, but I don't want her to suffer."

"Dogs have a high threshold for pain," Greenwell said, "but PJ is experiencing significant discomfort. You can tell by the arch in her back. She has transferred her weight from her back legs to her front legs. That causes her back to arch."

The vet asked me to move to the other side of the office and call PJ's name. I walked across the room. "PJ, come here, girl. Come, honey. Good girl. You are so pretty."

As PJ limped across the floor of the examination room, I noticed the way she favored her front legs.

"See how she walks across the room?" the vet said.

I nodded. "So, what do you think? Should we put her down?"

"No, not yet."

Greenwell and his assistant placed PJ on a hydraulic lift table that raised her to a more comfortable position. As PJ was lying on the table, there was a small wag from her tail.

"I would like to try something. I suggest we start her on Cosequin DS, a cartilage builder, and aspirin for her pain. Maybe I can reduce her pain and give you and PJ a few extra months together."

We started PJ on the medicine right away, and I hoped for the best. In a few days, her appetite returned; she gained three pounds in one week, and the pain in her hips lessened. Both Greenwell and I were happy with her progress and agreed we would continue the treatment. I was happy that she didn't have to be put down and that we could have a few more months together.

I began to relish the little things, such as sitting on the floor and stroking PJ's body while her head rested on my leg, the quiet walks in the backyard when PJ stopped and ate some birdseed laying on the ground, and the times when we watched an Illinois basketball game on the television and shared a bag of unshelled peanuts.

Most of all, I appreciated PJ's bad days, the days when she couldn't go up and down the stairs leading to our backyard. When I sensed that PJ needed to go outside, I carried all sixty pounds up and down the snow-covered stairs. On days when I thought PJ had reached the end, she would bounce back with a couple of good days. But after five months, PJ's bad days were almost every day.

It was a Monday afternoon when I returned from work and found PJ lying on the floor. She struggled to stand. I called Greenwell, and he said we could bring her in immediately.

My wife and I put PJ in our car. Except for the hum of tires rolling on the highway, the drive to the vet was quiet. When we arrived, PJ was too weak to even hop out of the car, so I lifted her in my arms again. Paula held the door to Greenwell's office open as I carried PJ inside. Greenwell's assistant was waiting for us as we entered and led us into the examining room. I placed PJ gently on the examination table. While we waited for Greenwell to arrive, Paula and I did our best to comfort PJ by stroking her back and telling her it was going to be okay. "We love you so much," we said. "We'll make the pain go away, PJ. We promise." We both knew this was the end.

A few minutes later, Greenwell entered and looked at PJ. "Yes, PJ's ready," Greenwell said. "We'll take her to the other room and insert a catheter in her leg. Then we'll bring her back so you can say your goodbyes."

"Can I go with you?" I asked.

"No, I'd rather you wait here. It'll be better this way. Trust me. We will be back in a few minutes."

PJ returned riding a metal cart that was covered with a soft rug. She lay on her side, but I could see the tension in her back. Her cropped ears lay flat, and a catheter was taped to her leg. Paula stood by PJ's head, I stood by her back paws, and Greenwell stood in between. Greenwell leaned forward and began to administer the drug. "Good girl, PJ," Greenwell said. "Your pain is almost over. You're such a good girl."

As the drugs entered her bloodstream, the arch in PJ's back disappeared, and she relaxed with a final sigh. A feeling of peace radiated throughout the room. Greenwell listened through the stethoscope for a heartbeat. "She's gone."

I looked at PJ's eyes which were still open, but I could see her dark irises were still.

It was September 10, 2014.

Months later, on the bank of a dry creek at the end of our property where the sun had pulled perennials through the topsoil, Paula and I planted a small ornamental tree. We used a mixture of topsoil and PJ's ashes. The tree, a slow grower, we were told, had smooth bark and limp branches of glossy oval leaves that draped like the canopy of an umbrella. The way the tree was positioned, it leaned slightly over the creek. A few pink blossoms floated to the ground as we stepped back to view the tree.

I turned to Paula. "Do you realize what kind of tree we just planted?"

My wife thought for a few seconds. "Oh my goodness. It's a weeping cherry tree."

Although I felt sadness, PJ's death was both beautiful and gentle. It was like my heart accepted two coexisting feelings—the emotions of a deep sadness accompanied by the belief that the soul passes from one life to another.

———

Less than two weeks later, I was working in my office on a Sunday, hoping to catch up on some unfinished business. The doors were locked, and the blinds were closed when I heard a soft knock on my window. I lifted the blinds. It was Russell, the grandson of John, an eighty-two-year-old man who lived next door to my office. John spent the summer afternoons sitting on his front porch watching the cars pass by and keeping an eye on a car wash across the street where he did custodial work. Oftentimes, I joined John on his front porch before driving home for the evening. There was never a lot of discussion between the two of us. Though he was twenty years older than me, it felt good to be around him. Words were unnecessary. Of course, there was the occasional comment about the weather, if the car wash had been busy, and how's your family. We shared a space in the universe, a mutual respect, and a quiet love.

Russell saw me through the window and gestured toward the door. I nodded, dropped the blinds, and opened the front door. "John just passed," Russell said. "Would you like to come over and see him?"

Except for the funeral home, I had not seen a dead person. Yet, I felt at ease with Russell's question. I nodded, "Yes, I would like that." As Russell and I left my office and walked across the lawn to John's home, I experienced a newfound feeling of love for John. His death felt like PJ's passing with the calm connected with grief. The similarity was stunning.

Inside, John's daughter, Ruby, greeted me and said they had cleaned John up and dressed him. "He's been close to death the past two weeks," she said. "I told him last night that it was okay for him to die. But he was concerned about me. I told him that I'd be fine. Then he died."

She led me to John's bedroom, where he lay on his bed dressed in his Sunday best. "He thought the world of you," Ruby said. "I'll leave you alone for a bit." She gestured to a chair next to his bed. "You can sit there and pray with him if you like." This was the first time I had ever seen a dead body since my dad's funeral, and the concept of praying with someone who had already passed away was unfamiliar to me, but I sat in the chair anyway.

The afternoon sun shone through a window, making John's dark skin look copper in the warm light. I studied his strong-looking face with deep-set wrinkles. He was a handsome man. I touched his skin. It was soft and slightly warm from the sun. I wondered if his soul was still in the room or if it had already gone to Heaven. Either way, I felt like I was witnessing a spiritual event. I had never felt this way about someone who had died—only my dogs—but I felt at peace sitting next to John, the one I called my friend.

Perhaps There's a Pill
for That

2000–2002
Makanda, Illinois

Robin Williams, John Belushi, Chris Farley, Freddie Prinze were all funny men who chose to die. They lacked any resolution to that harmonic pedal-point of misery—a can't-move sadness creating the illusion that death is more attractive than life. Not only does this illusion lurk in the darkness of night, the underbelly of a rotting rat, or the heart of a seven-year-old boy subjected to horrific abuses, it's everywhere. It is a formidable enemy we call depression.

My mother referred to depression as having a bad case of the nerves. "I'm having trouble with my nerves today," she often said. To me, depression feels heavy, like a cloud of tears; it's the darkness that yearns for a glimmer of light, a reason to get up in the morning, a promise from God that light overcomes darkness.

Causes of depression can be genetic makeup, physical and sexual abuse, conflict, death or loss, physical or emotional pain, reaction to medication, to name a few.

Some or all can contribute to a chemical imbalance in the brain, a misfiring of neurons that can bring you to your knees. Normally, when information is transferred from one neuron to another, the gap between the terminals and nearby neurons is filled by chemical substances called neurotransmitters which fire across the space, sending signals to other neurons, like tiny sparks of electricity. Imagine a well-lit midway at a county fair, with hundreds of rides and booths operating simultaneously.

There are some fifty different neurotransmitters in the brain, and too much or too little of these neurotransmitters may contribute to schizophrenia, depression, bipolar disorder, and other emotional conditions. When a person's neurotransmitters do not function properly, it is said they have a "chemical imbalance." Since communication between and among neurons dictates how our behavior is controlled, a chemical imbalance can impact how a person walks, raises an arm, sits on a stool, or orders a cup of coffee. Those of us suffering from depression are excruciatingly aware of its impact on our behavior, and we must regularly evaluate our actions against our perception of what is "normal." We are always trying to signal normal behavior to those around us.

I remember a certain day when I was barely fifteen. It was a time when Johnny Carson was the funny man of late-night television. Sitting in the isolation of my home, the idea entered my mind that I could become the next Johnny Carson. I seemed to have a talent for saying "witty" things, acting crazy, and making my friends laugh. An abuse victim needs tools for survival, and for me, those tools included humor, alcohol, and ongoing conversations with God. I can't speak for Robin Williams, John Belushi, Chris Farley, or Freddie Prinze, but for me, humor was a method of dealing with my misery. Just as in the wintertime, when the temperature hovered around zero degrees I didn't go outside without my coat, when depression was dark and heavy, I didn't go outside without my humor. But perhaps humor, by itself, can only keep the tormented soul from death for a time. Perhaps if I had not met Olivia, humor would not have been enough, and I would have died. Perhaps that is what happened to those other funny men.

Decades later, I asked my therapist if my humor was annoying and whether I should refrain from being "funny." She asked me to imagine myself without the humor and whether I liked that person. I quickly concluded that the imagined person was boring. She smiled before saying, "Hey, funny man. I like who you are."

Olivia suggested that I try medication to reduce my anxiety and depression, but I wanted to understand how it worked before I agreed. I learned that the medication, a pea-sized pill, moves through the body like a mouse through a maze. First, it is absorbed in the stomach, penetrates the lining of the intestines, and races through the bloodstream to its intended target—receptors on the surface of certain neurons in the brain. To achieve the intended effect, psychoactive drugs must bind to and interact with these receptors, changing the functional properties of that neuron and thus, paving the way for healthy, "normal" behavior. However, only a small portion of the medication is attached to the intended receptor in the brain at any given time. The rest of the drug languishes in other parts of the body, where it may cause unpleasant side effects before it is metabolized by the liver and excreted by the kidneys. The process is repeated until the desired level and duration of the drug is reached and a steady state of "chemical balance" is maintained.

Although pharmacology has made rapid strides since the middle of the twentieth century, it is not an exact science. Side effects from the drugs are not uncommon and sometimes require a period of trial and error to find the correct medication and dosage. My initial experience left me with side effects similar to a bad case of the flu. When I switched to a different medication, it eliminated the negative side effects but didn't reduce my anxiety. I agreed to try the original medication again and give my body more time to make the necessary adjustment. Fortunately, it worked. My depression and anxiety lessened, leaving me in a more receptive state of mind where I welcomed the therapy and medication that offered a better quality of life. Thoughts of suicide also decreased, though to be honest, I don't know if that was because of years of therapy or the fact that I was much older. Even now, as I approach eighty, the possibility, while very small, continues to provide me with a measure of control in my life. I suppose it will always be my ace-in-the-hole.

OKAY, GOD.
WHAT IS GOING ON?

Northwestern Memorial Hospital
Chicago, Illinois

By 2010, I had been in psychotherapy with Olivia for nearly seventeen years. It would be just two more years before my weekly sessions became monthly check-ins, but I had no way of knowing that at the time. By then, all my friends and family, including my general practitioner, knew I was in therapy and would periodically ask me how I was doing. When they did, my response typically consisted of some version of "It's difficult, but I'm making progress." So when my doctor called me into her office to go over the results from my annual blood test, I was not surprised when she asked how therapy was going. What she said next took me completely by surprise.

"While most of your tests are within the normal range for a man your age, your PSA numbers are high and a bit concerning. I would like to send you to a urologist for a biopsy of your prostate."

When a man my age hears the word prostate, his mind goes to one place. "Do you think I have cancer?" I asked.

The doctor was quick to reassure me. "Not necessarily. The biopsy is a tool to help determine if we have a problem. Our office will set up your appointment with the urologist who will perform the biopsy and go over the results with you."

A few days later, I went to the urologist's office, where a nurse did the biopsy and arranged for me to come back in a week and meet with the urologist. While I waited, I didn't allow myself to consider the possibility of cancer. Certainly not now when I was in therapy for childhood sexual abuse. After all the progress I had made to rebuild myself so that I could have a healthy sex life, and all the love and patience Paula had shown me in the process, the possibility that I would lose my ability to have an erection seemed totally unreasonable and certainly unfair.

A week later, I was sitting in another doctor's office, waiting for the news on my biopsy. When the urologist came in, I expected some getting-to-know-you chit-chat or a comment about the weather, at least. I got neither.

"Mr. Franklin, you have prostate cancer, and we need to remove your prostate. We can schedule your surgery for next week."

That was it. Wham, bam, you got cancer, man. *He can't always be this much of an asshole,* I reasoned. *Maybe he's running behind and needs to move on to his next appointment.* "Doctor," I said, "I need some time. There are things I need to know."

He ignored my opening for questions. "Larry, you are a good candidate for the surgery. We need to move forward. Prostate cancer is serious. If left untreated, you will die."

I pressed him. "If I have the surgery, will you be able to save the nerves around the prostate so I can continue having sex?"

The doctor seemed baffled by my question. He didn't know my situation and probably couldn't understand why I was so concerned about having sex.

"The urologic oncologist who will perform the surgery won't know if you need to have nerves removed until the surgery. Regardless, I'm confident that you will have a successful surgery and live a long life."

I appreciated his confidence in the oncologist's skill and my life expectancy, but it wasn't enough. I needed to know more. "Doctor, I need some time," I said.

"Mr. Franklin, we can give you a few days but don't ignore the problem. Call our office when you're ready to schedule an appointment," he said and left the room.

Time for another discussion with God.

Okay, God. What is going on? I continue to work on my recovery from sexual abuse, and I end up with prostate cancer. If it had to be cancer, why did you choose prostate cancer? This will affect my sex life. A mixture of sexual abuse and prostate cancer is a bit overwhelming. I just don't understand why this is all happening at the same time. God, are you wanting to destroy me? Is this some joke? While I don't mean to be disrespectful, are you sitting above the clouds laughing your ass off?

God didn't answer, so I went to my good friend, Jerry. He'd had surgery for prostate cancer a few years ago and was willing to share his experience with me. We met at the local coffee shop. He urged me to act quickly and not put off the surgery. Prostate cancer was no joke, and I could die from it. His recommendation was to go with Dr. Catalona, a renowned surgeon in Chicago who invented the PSA blood test for prostate cancer. Dr. Catalona was my best chance to save the nerves around my prostate and have a normal sex life.

"So what's sex like after surgery?" I asked Jerry.

"Your sex life changes," he said, "even if you keep all your nerves. During the first six months after surgery, you probably won't have a sufficient erection, so they give you this medication you inject into the side of your penis. It just takes a few minutes, and you can achieve an erection sufficient for sex." He smiled, "And beware of overdosing with the penile injections. I was looking to hit a home run one night and injected too much of the magical medication in my penis."

"What do you mean, too much? What happened? I don't want to die."

Jerry laughed and nearly spat his coffee across the room. "Now, don't freak out. You won't die. If you inject too much medication, your erection could last for several hours and possibly cause permanent damage to your penis."

Now my concern turned to curiosity. "So, what happened?"

"My wife took me to the ER. They took a long needle and drew blood from my penis. It gradually returned to its normal size."

"Oh my God. That had to be embarrassing. Your wife must have freaked out."

"Yes, it was embarrassing, and I won't do it again. The doctor told me that you could inject this medication into a corpse, and it would have an erection."

My mind immediately flashed back to the floating erection in my sewage dream. Jerry must have seen something in my face that worried him because he was quick to reassure me. "I'm sure the doctor was joking," he said. "You'll be okay. Just don't try to impress Paula with an extra-large penis."

I took Jerry's advice and arranged for surgery with Dr. Catalona.

The surgery was uneventful, and afterward, Dr. Catalona told me he had managed to save most of the nerves, but there was an area where the cancer was close to seeping out and into another part of my body. He had to shave off a few of the nerves in that place.

He told me it was a good thing I'd had the surgery when I did. "If you had waited a few more months, the cancer might have spread outside of your prostate, and that would have been bad. We'll keep an eye on it. You're going to be fine."

Several weeks later, I returned to see Dr. Catalona for a checkup. He said that everything looked good, and I could return in one year. Before he left the room, I asked him about penile injections that would enable erections. "Oh yes," he said. "I almost forgot. Let me prepare the injection, and then I'll show you how to do it."

Once the injection was prepared, Dr. Catalona told me to remove my pants, then he handed me a syringe filled with the magical medication. "Push the needle into the side of your penis."

I was probably looking a bit pale by now. "I don't think I can do this."

"Larry, trust me. This is going to be okay."

I carefully began pushing the needle into the side of my penis. Much to my surprise, the needle went in easily, and I was able to push the plunger, sending the medication into my penis. I withdrew the needle and placed it gently on a silver tray Dr. Catalona had ready for me. I was breathing hard and covered in a light sweat.

"You just wait here," Dr. Catalona said. "Let's give the medicine a chance to take effect. I'll be back in a few minutes."

Dr. Catalona left the room while I stood with my pants laying on the floor. Now, all I had to do was watch my penis and see if it moved. It didn't take long. In minutes my penis began to swell. Oh, my God! I can't tell you how exciting it was. I would be able to have sex again. My only concern was that I was still standing with my pants down and a penis that was about to salute. Should I pull my pants up? What if a nurse walked in? Just then, the doorknob turned. I fumbled for my pants but was unable to cover myself in time. Thank God it was only Dr. Catalona. He looked at my penis.

"Yes, that looks good," he said. "I'll have the drugs and syringes mailed to you. Let me know if you have any problems. See you in a year."

I left the hospital and crossed the street to a coffee shop where Paula said she would be waiting for me. I found her sitting at a corner table. We ordered some coffee, and she asked me how it went. "Is everything okay?" She seemed anxious.

"The checkup was fine, and Catalona wants to see me in a year. Now, let me tell you what really happened. It was absolutely fantastic, Paula. I took a syringe and injected some medication into my penis, and in a few minutes, it was actually growing. I'm not kidding. I got an erection right there in the office. In a week or so, I'll receive the syringes and medication in the mail. Then we can see how it works."

Paula didn't even try to hide the look of satisfaction on her face when she asked, "Did it hurt?"

"Yes, it hurts, but sometimes a man's gotta do what a man's gotta do," I said, laughing. The excitement for what this meant for Paula and me, coupled with the relief that I was not going to die from prostate cancer, made me do something that surprised both of us, but at the time, seemed like the most natural thing to do. I pushed back my chair, stood up, and turned to address the coffee shop. "Excuse me, ladies and gentlemen, but I have a brief announcement." I paused to give everyone time to turn from their coffee and conversation and face me. Once I had the attention of the room, I said, "My name is Larry Franklin, and I just had a radical prostatectomy for the removal of prostate cancer." I paused for dramatic effect. "I am now cancer-free."

Twenty-five strangers began applauding, and even though it wasn't because of anything I had done, the cheers felt good and well deserved. If I could recover from prostate cancer, then I could recover from abuse. I had been in therapy for seventeen years, and it was that day in a Chicago coffee shop when I felt that I could become emotionally healed.

THE STORY NEVER ENDS

September 2020
Flora, Illinois

In the fall of 2020, I was scheduled to give a presentation at a library in Flora, Illinois, a town with a population of 5,020 people and a mere seven-minute drive from my hometown. Since my presentations were advertised to the general public, there was the possibility that my cousins John or Sammy, the only living perpetrators of the physical and sexual violence against me, might show up. I always wondered how I would react if they did.

Sammy had been more of an observer who participated in a nonsexual way, and I didn't feel the need to confront him, though I was curious to know what he remembered. I'd always had a fear of confronting John, however, because of his violent nature. Regardless, I continued speaking at local venues, confident that I could handle any uncomfortable situation that might occur.

The event at the Flora library was scheduled for 2:00 pm. It was a small audience of about twelve people. Some I knew, and some I did not. John and Sammy

208 Larry L. Franklin

were not there. I introduced myself and began my talk, which I had presented more than a dozen times. Fifteen minutes into my talk, two more people entered the room and took seats in the back. It was Sammy and his wife. They smiled at me as I continued talking. While I felt a little uncomfortable, I was supported by the truth.

At the end of my talk, some of the people came forward to share their own experiences of abuse with me. I noticed that Sammy and his wife stood by, waiting their turn. When everyone else had left, Sammy asked his wife to give us some private time.

"When did all of this abuse happen?" he asked once she'd left the room. He asked the question so earnestly, as though he didn't know anything about it. It made me angry.

"What do you mean, 'When did this happen?' You know when it happened. You were there. You didn't participate in the sexual abuse, but you were there."

Sammy stepped back, an expression of shock on his face. Then he said, in a very different tone from before, "I sometimes wonder if John ever raped me."

"Are you telling me your brother raped you?" I asked.

"I don't know, but I wouldn't be surprised. I'd seen him do some bad stuff."

"Like what? What did you see him do?"

What happened next was similar to a conversation I had with a woman whose husband was incarcerated for murder. When she shared his story with me, she spoke of him in the third person, as if it were someone else who had committed murder, not her husband. As

Sammy began telling me his story about babysitting a young boy with his brother, he spoke of the young boy in the third person, as if the boy was not the man standing before him.

"We were babysitting a young boy whose parents had gone to a dance. The boy was about six or seven. Keith, John, and I were there."

I nodded. It was common for Keith, John, and Sammy to watch me while our parents attended the dances at Farmer City.

"Who was the little boy?" I asked.

"I don't know," Sammy said. "But I felt sorry for the boy. I've often wondered how that affected him. Wondered if he was all messed up."

"What happened?"

"My brother made the little boy give him a blow job. After John climaxed, he urinated in the little boy's mouth."

"Sounds like the little boy was me," I said.

Sammy didn't respond. While his story was one of the most horrific a man could imagine, it was the validation I had sought for years. This was proof that I was not crazy.

"Did anyone try to stop John?" I asked.

"No one did. You know John. He's as strong as a bull. I can't imagine what he would have done to me if I had tried. I was just shocked. I still wonder what happened to that little boy."

I probably could have learned more if I had continued our conversation, but an imaginary voice told me to leave. Sometimes things are so bad that you have to surface for air. Unfortunately, there wasn't a bathroom nearby, a place where I could grab hold of a stool and vomit.

———

Once I began writing my story with the intent to publish it, I began dreaming again. The dreams ranged from uncomfortable to horrific. Many were dreams of someone attacking me, causing me to kick and swing in my sleep. More than once, Paula was awakened by an elbow hitting her side or by my thrashing feet.

In time, my dreams changed from where I was the victim to where I was the attacker. Some nights I woke up crawling on the bedroom floor as if I was searching for something or someone. The worst dreams were episodes of screaming, intense fear, and flailing. In addition to emotional stress, they caused me physical harm. One night, I woke up at 3:00 am when my face crashed into the top of the wooden nightstand. I pulled myself out of bed and went to the bathroom mirror to see if I had sustained physical damage. When I flipped on the light, I saw a steady stream of blood running from my mouth and down my neck. The collar of my pajama top was spattered with blood. Upon inspection, I saw that one of my front teeth had cut through my upper lip. I grabbed a towel to press against my face and woke Paula.

"Paula, it's bad. I really messed up this time. I think I need to go to the ER."

She turned on the lights, saw my bloody pajama top and the bloody towel pressed to my face. "Oh my God, Larry! What happened?"

"I don't know. I woke up when my face crashed into the top of the nightstand. My front tooth is loose, though, and it cut through my lip. I guess it was caused by a bad dream. But I don't know what it was about."

Paula asked to see the damage, and when I pulled the towel away, she said my lip looked like a bloody chunk of beef. She drove me to the ER. It took ten stitches to sew my upper lip back together. I was fortunate to have an excellent surgeon who turned a chunk of battered flesh into a small scar on the outer part of my lip. In a few months, my front tooth tightened up, eliminating the need for a dental implant. But I have to be careful with my enunciation of certain words; my lips are now a bit lazy when I pronounce certain syllables.

Paula and I made changes in our sleeping arrangements to protect both of us. I moved to a separate bedroom where all furniture was removed except the bed, reducing any chance of hurting myself. Still, the risk was not eliminated. A couple of weeks later, I woke up after running full speed into the bedroom wall. Whether I was chasing someone or being chased in my dream, I don't know. Fortunately, no stitches were needed, but the incident left cuts and bruises on my face, giving me the appearance of having been beaten up.

This time, Paula insisted I see my doctor to find out what was wrong. I was told I was having night terrors, a symptom of my PTSD, and that I should not take them lightly. I was prescribed medication which I take every night before bed. That was six months ago, and I haven't had any additional night terrors.

As I come to the end of my book, I realize that I have not written anything about the passing of my mother.

She died on February 15, 2005, two days after Paula and I made what we knew would be our final visit. The nurse told me that it was a quiet passing.

It feels strange that I have left her death out of my manuscript. My mother opened the door, just a crack, to a place where repressed memories had lain hidden for decades. When I flung the door open, she refused to help me sort through anything I found. Her secrecy drove a wedge between the two of us that maybe had already been there, but which I became increasingly aware of in the last ten years of her life.

I don't remember my mother telling me that she loved me. And I only remember telling my mother once that I loved her. It may have been a lie, but like much of my past, I can never be absolutely certain.

My mother's health deteriorated during the last two years of her life. She went from living by herself to assisted living before we placed her in a nursing home. The home was one hundred miles from where Paula and I lived but close to where my mother had grown up. We expected her friends to visit her, but that never happened. Perhaps this was because she was ninety years old and most of her friends were dead. Still, she had been an active member of her church. There must have been someone from her church who could have visited her. I sometimes wonder if it was harder for my mother to hide the emptiness inside her the older she got. I wonder if others could see like I could that natural bonds of affection were impossible for her to cultivate.

While I managed to visit her most weekends, there were times when I couldn't—sometimes because of other commitments, sometimes because every trip challenged my sanity.

The trips were difficult. When Paula accompanied me, the conversation between my mother and me was less awkward, but if it was just me, it was awful. What do you talk about with a woman who has refused to talk with you most of her life? It helped if I visited during her dinner hour when we could talk about the food.

"How's the chicken? Is it tender?"

"It's not like my chicken. But you know, I like fried chicken better than baked."

"What about the peas? You like peas, don't you?"

"They're a little dry. I like them with more butter."

Once I'd asked her about everything on her plate, I'd move to dessert. "It says there's apple pie for dessert. That sounds good."

"It's not."

"They don't use that stuff out of a can, do they?"

"No, but they use the wrong kind of apples. And they cook them for too long. You can't cook apple pie for too long, or it gets soggy."

"Your apple pie was never soggy."

"Definitely not."

214 *Larry L. Franklin*

My mother took pride in her cooking and sewing skills. I remember a time many years ago when I bought her a hardcover sewing book for Christmas. It was full of detailed illustrations of complex techniques that I thought an experienced seamstress like my mother would cherish. When she opened the present, it was clear she was not pleased. That Christmas, I learned my mother had no interest in learning how others did something she was already an expert in.

When there were no meals to talk about, the silence would stretch from one excruciating minute to the next. During one of these visits, I asked her if she'd had any visitors.

"No one visits but you," she said.

"Really. What about your friends?"

"I don't have any friends. Guess they're all dead," she said.

"Have you made any friends here?" I ventured.

"No."

After a long pause, I asked, "Are you worried about dying?"

"No. I'm not worried about that," she snapped. Then she added softly, "I'm more worried about what I've done."

Her response took me by surprise. If it had been someone other than my mother, I would have jumped all over her statement, wanting to know more: "What do you mean 'what you've done'?" This honesty was so unlike her, I should have followed up, but I just sat there, unable to speak. Maybe I was afraid to hear what she would have said if I'd asked questions. I still wonder what she meant by her comment, *"I'm more worried about what I've done."*

In the final year of her life, my mother's condition deteriorated to the point where she only spoke in gibberish. On weeks when I couldn't make the trip to see her, I would call the nursing home and ask them to place my mother on the phone. When I would speak to her, she would answer in gibberish. I didn't know if she understood anything I said, but I persevered. But one day, when she spoke in gibberish, I answered in gibberish. This went on for the entire 10 to 15-minute call. Now we were on equal ground; neither of us understood what the other was saying. Afterward, I felt ashamed of my behavior and never did it again.

On my last visit, just as I was beginning to leave, my mother grabbed hold of my shirt and refused to let go. It was as if she were begging to go home with me. The tension between what I should do and what I could do was unbearable. The right thing would have been for me to take her to my house, but I didn't want to. Even if I'd wanted to, there was no way I could have. While the physical care would have been difficult, the emotional care would have been impossible. Given our history, the sexual abuse, secrets, and not protecting me as a child, I couldn't help her. I had to protect myself. I pulled away from her and escaped to my car.

A few weeks later, a nurse called and said that my mother was about to die, and I might want to see her before she passed. My wife made the two-hour trip with me but waited in the hall outside my mother's room while I went in. My mother lay in her bed, and while she was unable to speak, when she looked at me, it was obvious there was still some life left in her eyes. But I couldn't tell if she would understand anything I said. I left the room. Paula, who was sitting in a chair outside the door, stood up.

"How is she?" Paula asked.

"I don't know. She seems the same to me." I paused. "I didn't know what to say, so I left. You want to go in? I just need some time to think."

Paula nodded and went in to say her final words to my mother. When she came out a few minutes later, I didn't ask her what she said.

Now it was my turn.

I went back in and was struck by the sameness of the room: stale, plain, and lifeless colors that signaled a death that had come or was about to come. I was uncertain if my mother was thinking or if her mind was void of any cerebral activity. I imagined she was laying on a conveyor belt waiting to be moved to a different place. Her death would activate the belt, moving her body to a fork in the road where she would travel to the right or to the left. I wondered which way she might go. I could only speculate.

I approached my mother's bed. I held her hand and looked into her eyes. Her hand was warm, but her eyes were cold. I felt something powerful in me; I wasn't sure what it was, but I knew what to say. It was a lie. Well, I think it was a lie: "Mom, I love you. Enjoy your life in Heaven."

I turned and walked away.

EPILOGUE

After my mother's death, aunts, uncles, cousins, and close friends of my mother ostracized me. I first noticed I was being shut out when I no longer received the letters at Christmas where people list all the good things that have happened in their life over the past year. Next came the reduction in Facebook friends, followed by the absence of phone calls and invitations to family reunions.

Life is a bit lonely.

Not long ago, my youngest granddaughter was visiting Paula and me. She was in our bedroom, chatting, and her attention turned to the pictures on the wall. One of our bedroom walls is filled with photos of my wife's family. My wall is blank. My granddaughter pointed to the blank wall and asked, "Pop, why don't you have any photos of your mom or your dad or your brother?"

"I gave them to your mom and Aunt Teryl so they could enjoy them," I said. It was the truth, but not the whole truth.

My grandchildren are the only ones who don't know my story. Maybe someday, when they are old enough to read my memoir, they will discover who Pop was.

I hope they will understand.

Acknowledgments

Every writer needs someone to make their dream come true. For me, it was Karen Gowen, Owner and Managing Editor for WiDo Publishing and E. L. Marker. Gowen and her staff brought *Victims Make the Best Birdhouses* to fruition. A special thanks to Jay Christopher, Acquisitions Manager for E. L. Marker Publishing Company. Jay's remarkable skillset and his empathy for my lifelong struggles created a caring relationship between the two of us. We spent a year examining the manuscript as if we were looking for a vaccine that would save the world. Together, the efforts created the best of my writing.

This book would not have been possible without my therapist, Janet Coffman, PhD. How can I thank someone for saving my life? Janet brought me back from a man without a soul to someone capable of feeling.

There have been others who offered their support. Charlette McCloud taught me the benefits of meditation while the owners of Wilderflowers showed me how to communicate with the flowers. Elizabeth Klaver and Lisa Knopp launched my writing career while Diana Hume George, Patsy Sims, Thomas French, and Leslie Rubinkowski, were instrumental in my pursuit of the MFA degree in Creative Nonfiction at Goucher College in Baltimore, Maryland. This is where my first book was born.

I must acknowledge Amy Somers, a Licensed Professional Counselor and fellow student in the Goucher MFA program, who can change a rainy day into one filled with sunshine. Amy read my manuscript and convinced me to share it with the world.

There was an emotional cost in writing my memoir, demanding time for my soul to recharge. A special love for my wife, Paula, and her support and understanding when my mind went down a different road. We are currently celebrating the fifty-fourth year of our marriage. Life is good.

About the Author

Larry L. Franklin holds bachelor's and master's degrees in music and performed in the U. S. Navy Band located in Washington, D.C. from 1967 to 1971. From 1972 through 1975, Franklin taught music at Southern Illinois University. In 1976, he completed requirements for a certified financial planner designation and maintained a successful investment business.

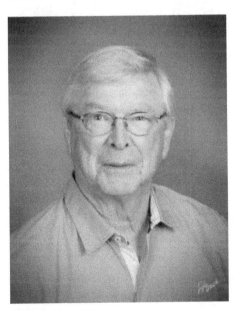

CPSIA information can be obtained
at www.ICGtesting.com
Printed in the USA
JSHW041921270522
26332JS00007B/189

9 781947 966567